W9-AHG-920

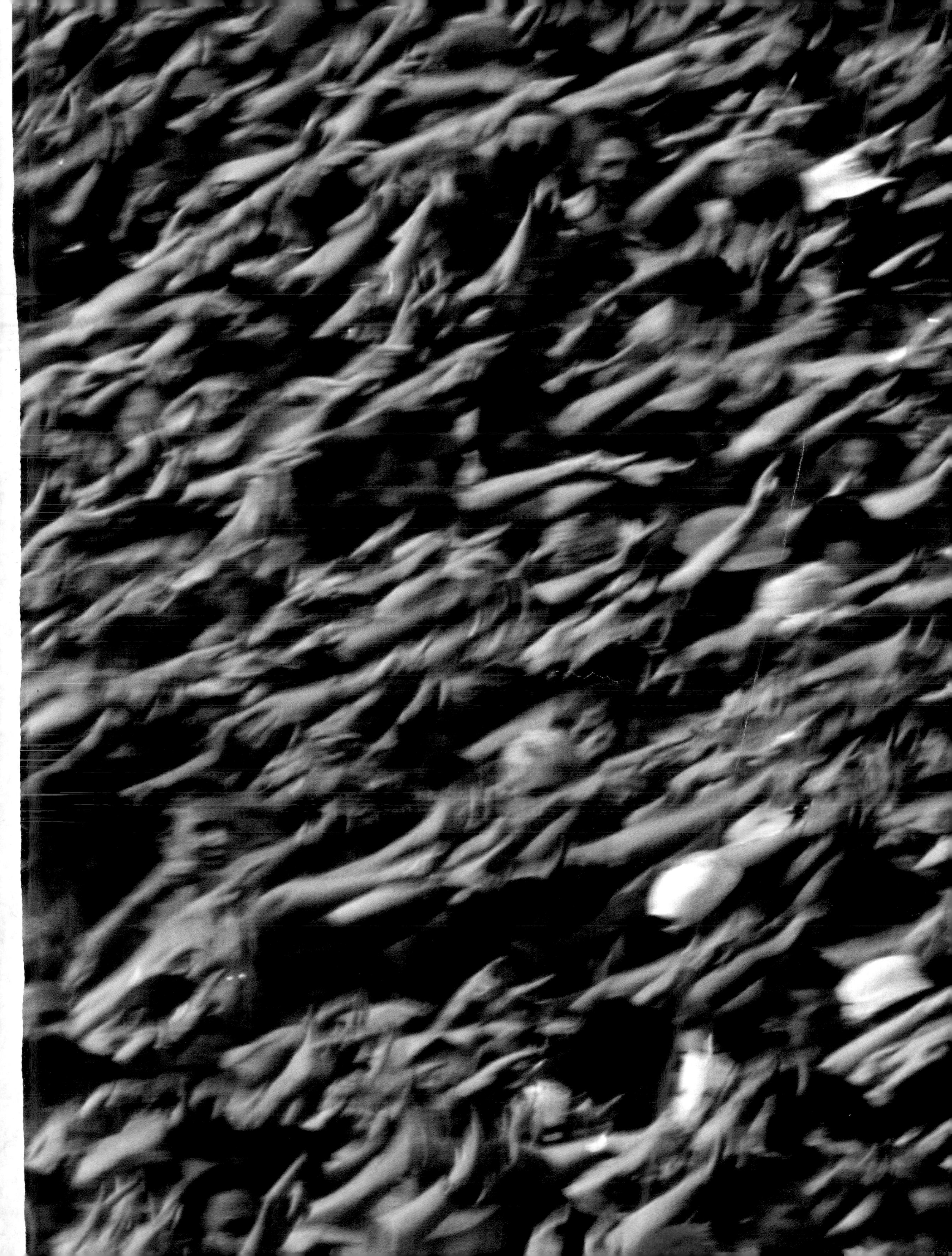

FOOTBALL AMERICA

Celebrating Our National Passion

FOREWORD BY DON SHULA

TEXT BY PHIL BARBER AND RAY DIDINGER

IN ASSOCIATION WITH THE NATIONAL FOOTBALL LEAGUE

TURNER PUBLISHING, INC.
ATLANTA

FOOTBALL AMERICA
Celebrating Our National Passion

Published by Turner Publishing, Inc.
A Subsidiary of Turner Broadcasting System, Inc.
1050 Techwood Drive, N.W.
Atlanta, Georgia 30318

Produced by National Football League Properties, Inc.
Publishing Group
6701 Center Drive West, Suite 1111
Los Angeles, California 90045

Library of Congress Cataloging-in-Publication Data
Barber, Phil.
Football America: celebrating our national passion/text by Phil Barber and Ray Didinger; foreword by Don Shula.—1st ed.
p. cm.
ISBN 1-57036-297-1 (alk. paper)
1. Football. 2. Football—Pictorial works. I. Didinger, Ray. II. Title.
GV951.B26 1996
796.332'0973—dc20 96-17341
CIP

The Photographers
Eric Lars Bakke: 16-17, 22-23, 25, 28-29, 81; Roger Ball: 56-57, 106; Vernon J. Biever: 18; Dave Black: 13; Mark Brettingen: 168, 172-173; Timothy Alan Broekema: 5; Peter Brouillet: 52, 244; Rob Brown: 185, 187, 188-189; D.E. Cox: 100; Greg Crisp: 110-111, 139; Scott Cunningham: 14, 192; Doug Devoe: 138; David Drapkin: 40, 84-85; Duomo: 1; Gerald Gallegos: 15, 248; David Martin Graham: 175; Peter Gridley: 180-181; Jon Hayt: 144, 166, 178-179, 206-207, 234, 235; Michael C. Hebert: 128; Thearon Henderson: 136; Paul Jasienski: 230-231; Catherine Karnow: 30-39; Mark Kelly: 58-71; Greg Le Boeuf: 226, 227; Al Messerschmidt: 46, 47, 53, 54-55, 75, 78-79, 80, 114-115, 137, 174, 194, 199, 228-229, 238-239, 256; Frank Micelotta: 148-153; Peter Read Miller: 74, 184, 189, 236; Tom Miller: 42, 48-49, 72, 146-147; Robert F. Moldaner: 117; Mike Moore: 82-83; Bill Mount: 21; Steven Murphy: 102; Joe Patronite: 12, 26-27, 87-99, 131, 145, 204, 237, 246-247; Joe Poellot: 196-197; Joe Robbins: 6; Bob Rosato: 20, 104-105, 109, 116, 118-125, 134-135, 171, 205, 240-241, 243, 245; G.B. Rose: 250-251; Todd Rosenburg: 126-127; Manny Rubio: 160-165, 176-177; Darrell Sandler: 169; Paul Spinelli: 247; Brian Spurlock: 107, 170; Tim Steinberg: 198; David Stluka: 108, 202-203, 208-223; Kevin Terrell: 113, 195, 253, 254-255; Al Tielemans: 103, 112, 130, 200-201; Tami A. Tomsic: 154-159, 252-253; Greg Trott: 139-140; Mark Trousdale: 132-133; Jim Turner: 19, 76-77, 182-183, 232-233; John Terence Turner: 24; Ron Veseley: 43, 44-45, 50-51, 142-143; Brian Wallace: 10; Laura Wilson: 2, 86; Baron Wolman: 224, 242.

CONTENTS

13

The Season Can't Start Soon Enough

By Don Shula

Let me tell you a story about myself—and about football. I played junior-high football in the ninth grade, and at the end of the season the coach took the best players from our squad and gave them a chance to play for the varsity. I was fortunate enough to get a tryout. In one of the early varsity practices I made a tackle, and in the process, cut my nose severely. I still have a scar from it. When I got home, my mom asked me what happened. I told her, and she said, "Okay that's it—no more football for you."

So that was the end of my football career—at least, my mom thought it was. I faked my parents' signatures on the permission slip the next fall. When they eventually realized I was playing, I persuaded them to put aside their reservations and go to a game. They watched me return a punt for a touchdown. From that moment on, they were my biggest fans. They never missed another game.

I guess that's why, like a lot of people in this country, I came to see football as a family event. I shared the game with my parents, just as I later shared it with my sons, Dave and Mike; and my daughters, Donna, Sharon, and Annie.

I got my boys involved in youth football, and I took them to all of my Miami Dolphins practices when they got old enough. Every Saturday before a game, we had a traditional family day—a loose practice to which you could bring your kids. They'd have their game going on one field, and

◀ Don Shula congratulates Dan Marino after a record-setting touchdown pass.

we'd be getting our team ready to play the Bills or the Steelers on the other field.

I attended a lot of Dave's and Mike's high school games, too—in the stands or, even better, walking along the sidelines. It was a real treat to be able to watch my sons compete in a sport that meant so much to me. Besides that, I loved the atmosphere at those games. Everything was well organized and the competition was good, yet there still was something very innocent about it.

Football has been part of my life for some 55 years. My earliest memory of the game—my earliest team photo—is from grade school. I went to a Catholic school, and I played on the fifth- and sixth-grade teams. It was seven-man touch football. We had two backs and five linemen, and that was it. That was where I first had to learn the skills of the game. It was my introduction to team sports, and I thoroughly enjoyed it.

Of course, there were painful moments, too. I remember we played in the championship game one year, and it brought my first losing experience, and the disappointment that goes with it. I was so upset after the loss that I hid behind the stands while my parents searched for me.

I had a good high school career in Painesville, Ohio, but I had the bad luck to graduate at about the time all the veterans were getting back from World War II. The college football programs were going after them, and I almost was left out. I couldn't have gone to college without a scholarship, and I ended up with just one offer—from John Carroll, a Jesuit university in Cleveland. It was a partial scholarship that paid my tuition; if I performed well, I would get room and board the next year, which I did. Until I got that partial scholarship, my intent had been to work for a year, and hopefully get enough money to go to school the next year. Well, "next year" never comes for many students in that situation, so I guess I have football to thank for my college education.

I was fortunate to attend John Carroll, which was right there in the shadow of the Cleveland Browns. My college coach, Herb Eisele, had a small staff, but he and his assistants went to every clinic ever staged by Paul Brown, the great Cleveland coach, and they watched the Browns practice right from the start of the franchise in 1946. So even at a small school like John Carroll, I was taught the fundamentals of the Cleveland Browns' playbook.

When the Browns drafted me in the ninth round in 1951, it was the fulfillment of a dream. I had grown up in the Browns' backyard, and my early idols had been Otto Graham (as a player) and Paul Brown (as a coach). To report to training camp and stand on the same field as Brown and Graham was just incredible. I was wide-eyed about the whole experience. As it turned out, I was the only rookie to make the team that year, and I actually started most of the games that season after the starting right cornerback got hurt early in the fall.

I suppose my story is pretty well documented after that: seven seasons with the Browns, the Baltimore Colts, and the Washington Redskins, after which I retired with 21 interceptions; being hired by the Colts as the youngest head coach (33) in NFL history in 1963, and taking them to the Super Bowl five years later; five more Super Bowls and two championships in 26 seasons with the Dolphins; a total of 347 NFL victories, which surpassed even the legendary George Halas of the Chicago Bears.

I feel blessed to be able to leave such a legacy. Football has been my passion, and a source of tremendous highs and lows. The biggest disappointment in my coaching career was Super Bowl III, when my Colts were upset by Joe Namath and the Jets. It was a bitter pill to swallow. Fortunately,

I've always been a guy who could learn from a negative experience and then move on—rather than being consumed by it.

My highest moment was Super Bowl VII. It was my first Super Bowl victory, and it capped a 17-0 season for my Dolphins. I admit that I had some trepidation the night before the game. I couldn't stop thinking that if something went wrong and we didn't win, we'd be 16-1—which would amount to a darned good season for most people. But it would have been a disaster for the Dolphins, and especially for me. A loss to the Redskins would have made me 0-3 in Super Bowls, and I didn't want to be associated with a record like that. Fortunately, we prevailed.

Nothing compares to the feeling of a big football game. Usually you can sense the excitement and the anxiety the minute you arrive at the stadium, even if it's two hours before kickoff. It's there in the pregame warmups and the National Anthem, too. It was there at each of my six Super Bowls and it was there in 1985, when the Bears roared into Miami with a 12-0 record and we had a chance to knock them off (and preserve the '72 Dolphins' place in NFL history). I'll never forget that night. The crowd was charged with electricity. The guys who had played on the 17-0 team were hanging around the sidelines, trying to do whatever they could to get our players ready to play. It worked: We beat Chicago 38-24.

That game demonstrated the emotional aspect of football, but what always intrigued me about the sport was the combination of the mental and the physical. I think the physical nature of football is what truly captures the imagination of the fans. There's a controlled violence on the field. And the great skills the game requires—the running, the throwing, the catching, and the defending—can be awesome.

And yet, with 11 people on each side, and with such a great variety of formations and plays, physical skills aren't enough. You also must be very intelligent to play the game. Paul Brown always said, "Football is a game of error...whoever makes the fewest errors wins."

The interesting thing is, the good players today are the same sort of guys who were good when I played, and in my early days of coaching. They're the players who are willing to expend every ounce of themselves to prepare for competition. You have to be disciplined; you have to work hard. There are no shortcuts to excellence in football, and there never will be.

I guess that's why training camp never was a curse to me. I've always likened the start of football season to going to some grand event, like a heavyweight boxing match or even a circus. In those situations, I find that the closer I get to the arena, the faster I walk. Sometimes you just can't wait to get in your seat. That's the way I am about the football season.

Don't get me wrong—I thoroughly enjoyed my offseasons. That was family time. June was always a happy month because that was when we vacationed. But near the end of June, or maybe the Fourth of July, I'd be overcome by the feeling that training camp was right around the corner.

I couldn't wait to get started.

That always was one of the measures I used to gauge my own desire. The minute I lost that anxiety, the minute the butterflies didn't invade my stomach when the ball was being kicked off to start a game, that was when I would look for something else to do. But guess what? In all my years in football, the feeling never left.

That sense of anticipation and excitement is what I'll remember and cherish. It's what I'll miss the most. I already do.

CHAPTER ONE

ALL-AMERICAN GAME

In 1990, scientists at the National Aeronautics and Space Administration (NASA) used an orbiting satellite's wave-length infrared technology to arrive at the following conclusion: The center of our galaxy is shaped like a football. ✯ Unexpected? Uh, yes. Still, some of us weren't a bit surprised to learn that the core of the Milky Way bears a striking resemblance to Paul Tagliabue's favorite signature pad. For years our lives have revolved around the game of football like spiraling arms composed of card stunts, Super Bowl parties, and autumn leaves crackling underfoot. ✯ Surveys tell us the NFL is the most popular professional sports league in America; Nielsen tells us it's the champion of TV ratings; sales of licensed products reflect the country's fascination with the game. But all of that says little about the extent to which football has permeated our culture. How has it happened? Why did a game once played only by brutes and obscure collegians evolve into an institution as warmly embraced as VCRs and fast food? ✯ Maybe part of the answer lies in the football's peculiar shape. ✯ When used with efficiency and power, the curious ellipsoid assumes a self-centered grace. Measure it, weigh it, and you're amazed at how far and accurately it can travel with human propulsion. But a football on the bounce is the definition of utter chaos. It is a dancing electron, a drunken acrobat. It sometimes looks as if it is possessed. ✯ Grace and chaos are the antagonistic forces that define the game of football. The images we associate with the sport are shaped by those contradictions. We see children crouching in a cow pasture, the tallest one telling the others to "just go deep." We see a high school team running wind sprints in August, a chasm of conditioning having separated the fit from the chubby. We see Joe Montana leading the 49ers—or the Chiefs, or Notre Dame—to a frenzied, huddleless comeback in the rectangular glow of a television set. ✯ Football is a postmodern cultural icon, not only a marker of seasonal passage but a means of transmitting the values of the nation. We know that football, substituting for the wars of previous (and less fortunate) generations, teaches preparation, teamwork, and effort—those most American of values. We've heard the words so often they have lost their weight, but 10,000 teachers, cops, and CEOs will point to a scarred knee or a bent finger and attest to the legitimacy of the cliché. There are less overt lessons, too: using guile to overcome physical inferiority; absorbing criticism without forfeiting pride; and accepting dumb luck as a major contributor to any outcome. ✯ And beyond virtue, there is tradition. A father throws down-and-outs to his 8-year-old daughter in the backyard. A bundled family sets a half-dozen seat pads on the aluminum benches of a high school stadium, ensuring a clear

◄ A GAME FOR ALL AGES...AND ALL WEATHER CONDITIONS. JUNEAU, ALASKA.

8

view of the eldest son when he takes the field. A group of giddy, graying fans, dressed cap to toe in red, gather for a pregame picnic at the University of Nebraska homecoming game, as they have annually for 30 years. They are snapshots of football in America, but they are reflections of community and custom. ✯ Football even has become part of a cherished holiday, seeping into the Thanksgiving ceremony as thoroughly as gravy on a hot plate of mashed potatoes. We all know what we have to be thankful for on that indulgent November day: companionship, the health of our loved ones, and Barry Sanders rushing for 158 yards. ✯ Not to view the sport entirely in soft focus. Steve Owen, who played in the NFL's primordial age and later coached the New York Giants for 23 seasons, once said, "Football was invented by a mean son of a bitch." ✯ He had a point. The game is infuriating and intense, and at the higher levels it is unquestionably violent. But football's mythic inventor had his poetic side, too. There is beauty in the game—in the uniforms and the pageantry, but also in the concerted movement of the players. ✯ This book is built on visual imagery, and so, in a way, is our appreciation of football. Play this sequence in your mind: A football is in the air, arcing in slow motion, blurring the background that frames it. There is a slight wobble to the rotation of the ball. It looks as if it were injured on the play, but somehow it found renewed determination. ✯ As the ball begins its inevitable descent, a world of possibility comes into focus at its end point. In one second a receiver will blindly obey his neurons and make the catch in a desperate horizontal stretch, or a safety will explode into the picture from an unseen angle to deny the completion, or the ball will flutter and ricochet off colliding players, chaos again acknowledged as the actors are pulled down by the order of gravity. ✯ Before that second has elapsed though, there is a fleeting instant of pure suspension, of serene temporary amnesia, when your heart seems to be running on a treadmill and you feel as though you are levitating. And the 100 or 5,000 or 100,000 people surrounding you in the stands are captivated by precisely the same experience, and they don't even know you exist. ✯ Priceless moments such as these breathe life into the day's waking hours. They are the moments that whisk you away from your complications and hardships and make you think: Man, I love this galaxy.

▲ A Stealth Bomber spies on Army and Air Force. Colorado Springs, Colorado.

◀ A grand entrance sets the mood for the big game. Dallas, Texas.

A WIDE-EYED REDSKINS FAN…

…AND A WILD-EYED RAIDERS ROOTER.

Forested hills and football practice in wine country. St. Helena, California.

Tiny Port Washington, Wisconsin, comes to a standstill for homecoming festivities.

The towering New York skyline stands oblivious to practice in Weehawken, New Jersey.

A perfect pass finds a receiver on the balmy beaches of Key West, Florida…

…and in the heat of an NFL battle between Arizona and Carolina.

Just go deep. Denver, Colorado.

WEEKEND WARRIOR. SEATTLE, WASHINGTON.

Snow flurries for the Broncos and the Chiefs in Denver, Colorado.

GOING AIRBORNE ON THE *U.S.S. GEORGE WASHINGTON*, OFF THE COAST OF VIRGINIA.

767

Moments before kickoff at North Dakota: Bowed heads and private thoughts.

Eric Benson warms up before the big game.

SAN MARIN, CALIFORNIA

The equipment was set out the night before. The jerseys, the pads, and the pants were stacked neatly on the bedroom floor.

The van was ready. Cathy Benson and her daughter Jennifer decorated it with green and gold streamers and filled the back with balloons. Cathy wrote "Go Ponies" on the windows with white shoe polish.

It was game day, and the San Marin Ponies were about to play for the 1995 championship of the Redwood Empire Football Conference. The Bentons were psyched.

Jimmy Benson, 11, was a fullback and defensive end for the Ponies, and Eric, 9, was an offensive guard. The Ponies had a 10-1 record, and, if they won this game, they would advance to the Pop Warner regional championships in Reno, Nevada. A victory there would mean a trip to the organization's Super Bowl in Orlando, Florida.

"We were a soccer and swimming family until Jimmy took up football, then we all got into it," Cathy says. The family lives in Novato, California, north of San Francisco.

"Jennifer [13] is a cheerleader for the Midget team. Eric signed up to play on the team with Jimmy. Our weekends became all football. It is hectic sometimes, but we love it."

The scene at the Benson house—"Hey, Dad, can you help me with my hip pads?"—is played out each autumn weekend in thousands of homes across the United States, Mexico, and even Japan.

More than 1 million youngsters between the ages of 7 and 16 take part in youth football, with coaches and hundreds of thousands of volunteers.

It's a kid's game, in the purest sense. That's why Jimmy and Eric Benson play it. That is why they get up at 6 A.M. on Sunday and wriggle into those bulky uniforms.

"It's the hardest game to play because there's all the hitting and you have to learn plays and stuff," Jimmy says. "But it's the most fun game to play, too.

"I like soccer, but when I went out for football, I liked that more. In football, you're doing something on every play. It's not like other sports, like baseball, where you just stand around."

Eric enjoys the game, too, even though as an offensive lineman he does all the dirty work and gets very little glory. He enjoys the competition. He loves to win.

"Eric has that fire in his belly," his mother says. "He is younger and smaller than most of the boys he plays against, but he blocks them anyway."

On the morning of the championship game, the Ponies followed their normal routine. All 35 players and their families met coach Ed Paulmenn at the oak tree in front of San Marin High School.

THE BENSONS ARE A FOOTBALL FAMILY, AS ERIC'S ROOM ATTESTS.

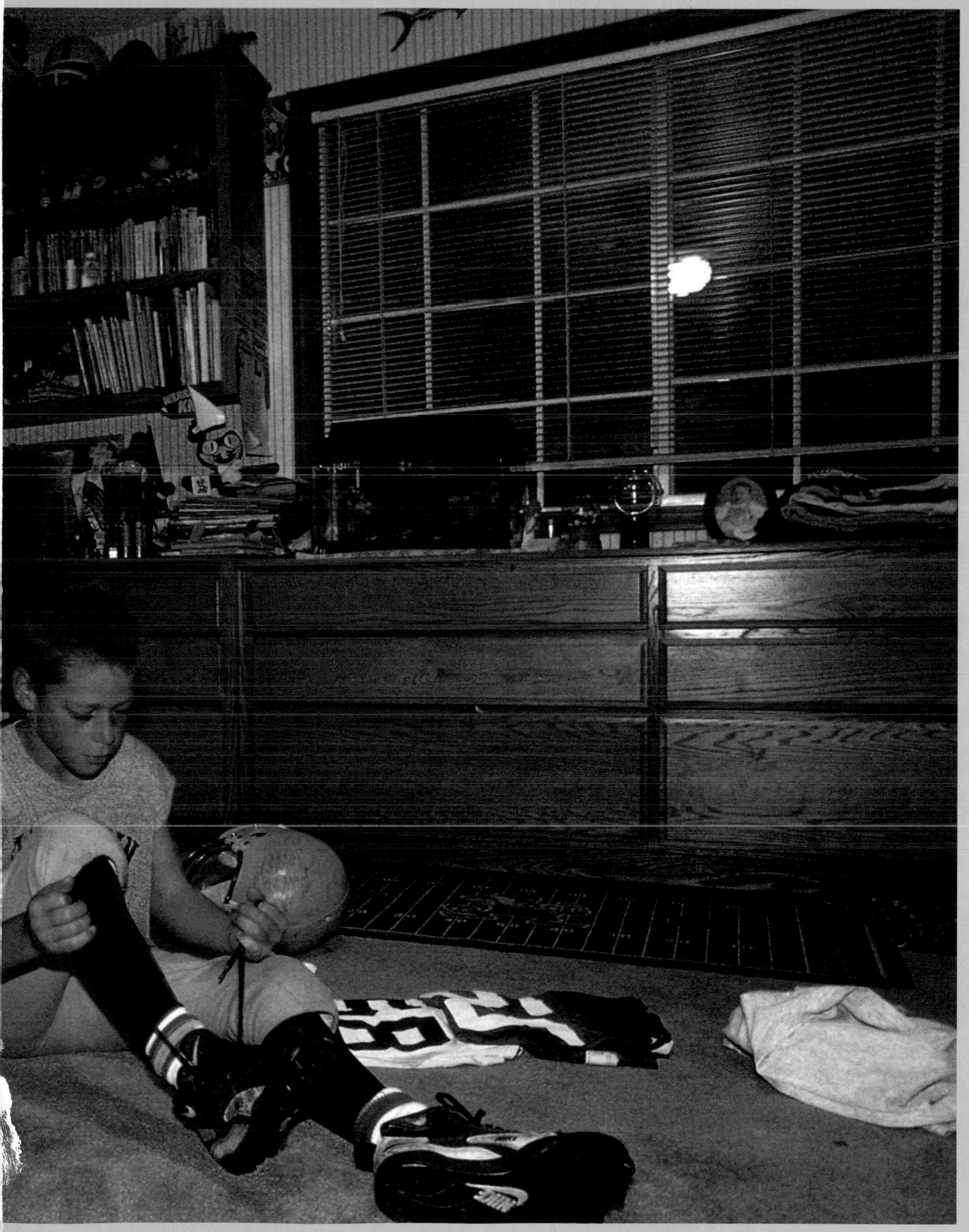

◀ JIMMY AND ERIC GET THEIR PREGAME MEAL.

There, Paulmenn counted heads and made sure everyone had directions to the field. The game was scheduled to be played in Napa, an hour's drive away.

The Ponies' opponent was the Ukiah Lions, the same team that defeated them in the 1994 conference final. The procession of cars and RVs, most decorated in the San Marin team colors, rolled off into the morning fog.

Jimmy and Eric sat in the back seat along with Jennifer. Cathy rode up front while husband Jim drove. The boys passed the time playing video games and arguing about who had the better trading-card collection.

"It was like a typical ride to anywhere," Cathy says. "I thought they might be nervous, but they weren't. You would've thought we were going to the mall."

When the Bensons arrived at the field, the first thing Jimmy noticed was the crowd, which was larger than usual. The stadium was bigger, too.

"It was exciting," he said. "I liked it."

All players have to weigh in before games. For Junior Peewees, the weight limit is 90 pounds to start the season. That limit goes up one-half pound a week, allowing the players to fill out.

As one of the younger players, Eric had no trouble making weight. Jimmy did, however. He had to sacrifice—goodby candy, hello rice cakes—to keep his weight down.

The strict adherence to age and weight limits was one reason Cathy and Jim Benson allowed their sons to play. They knew they did not have to worry about Jimmy or Eric being at risk playing against much bigger boys.

That is one reason why, in a survey conducted by the U.S. Consumer Product Safety Commission, organized football proved to be a safer activity for youngsters ages 5 to 15 than either

skateboarding or riding a bicycle.

"Safety is one of the main concerns," Cathy said. "I have no fears at all. The boys have the best equipment and the coaches teach them proper technique. They work really hard on conditioning. Our kids have two weeks of running and stretching before they start to hit."

Another selling point for parents is the attention to academics. A youngster must be a student in good standing to participate, either as a player or a cheerleader

Both Jimmy and Eric were Pop Warner Academic All-Americas in 1995. As a team, the San Marin Ponies had a 3.2 grade-point average, the best in the conference.

"Most of the kids' grades go up during the season," said Paulmenn, who has coached youth football for five years. "People who don't know would think the opposite, that the kids would be more distracted or tired and it would hurt them in school.

"These kids are sharper than that. What we do, through this program, is make them more responsible. I tell them right at the start, 'You're student-athletes. You have to keep your grades

up, you have to keep your bedroom clean, you have to do what's asked of you.'

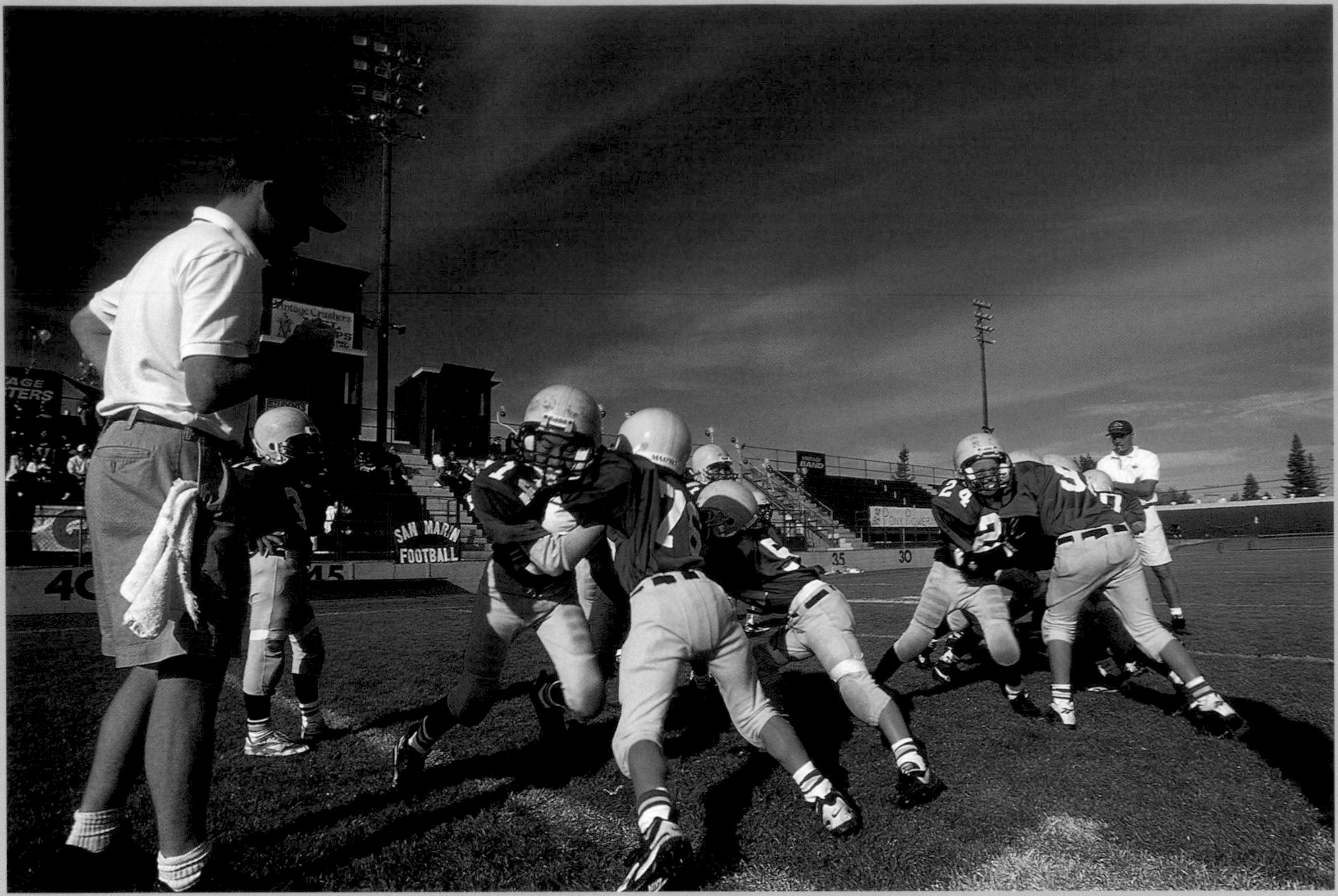

"I tell our kids, 'If you can't take care of that part of your life, then you can't play football. At least not with the Ponies.'"

In Pop Warner football every player who is dressed for a game must play at least four plays. If a team has fewer than 25 players, the minimum number of plays goes up to eight.

"The ability level is all over the map," Paulmenn said. "We have some kids who can really play and others who can't. Some kids really know football, others start out knowing almost nothing about the game.

"We start by handing out play sheets and diagramming formations on a board. Some kids say: 'This is football? It's more like school.' But once they start learning, they get excited. They want more and more.

"By the end of the season, they're talking about trap plays, line stunts, and cross-blocks. For me, that's the exciting part, watching these kids develop and come together as a team."

As San Marin piled up the victories in 1995, Paulmenn did his best to ensure that everyone shared in the team's success. Jimmy Benson did not have a touchdown in the first 10 games, so that was one of the team goals in the playoffs.

In the first playoff game, Paulmenn called a fake reverse with Jimmy carrying the ball. He turned the corner and outran the entire defense, going 50 yards for the touchdown that sparked the Ponies' victory.

Before the Ponies took the field for the championship game, the coaches smeared lamp black

under the eyes of each player. Earlier in the season, the coaches used it only on players who handled the ball, but because it gave the kids such an emotional charge, Paulmenn and his assistants decided to paint the whole team.

"It was like putting on a game face," Paulmenn said. "Each team has its own personality. Some are loud and boisterous. This group was real quiet. They'd be together before a game and you wouldn't hear a peep.

"I was looking for a way to get them fired up, and putting the black on their faces did the trick. We'd put it on them before the game; the kids would look at each other and start screaming and butting heads. It was better than a pep talk."

The Ponies played well in their championship game, but not well enough. They lost 6-0 to Ukiah, and the Lions went on to play in Super Bowl Week in Florida.

It was a disappointing finish to the season, and some of the San Marin players had tears in their eyes as they watched the Ukiah team accept the championship trophy.

Jimmy and Eric were down, but they got over the feeling in a hurry. By the time Cathy and Jim reached them for a postgame hug, Eric already

had other things on his mind, like eating.

Ten minutes later, the whole family was at the drive-through window at Taco Bell. Jimmy and Eric each had an order of nachos in his lap, and they were talking about what they wanted to watch on TV when they got home.

"I was sorry we lost. I would've liked to go on, but we did our best," Jimmy said. "We didn't play as good as we could have, but we played hard. We had fun all season. That was just one game."

"I talked to the kids after the game and told them how terrific they were," Paulmenn said. "I

told them they didn't have any reason to hang their heads.

"They played a good team, played them very tough and just came up short. That's football. That's life. I told them I was proud of how far they had come as individuals and as a team.

"The great thing about this kind of league is that nobody ever really loses. Every kid who plays gains something. The coaches, too."

of the Kansas City Chiefs or the Philadelphia Eagles. The stands could be empty, the only crowd noise could be the chirping of crickets, and still the players would swear and block and tackle as if it were Madden and Summerall calling the game. Once the opening kick is pinwheeling in the air, once an opponent thumps you in the chest with a forearm, that's it. You're involved. No matter what your frame of mind was before the game, the qualities that make you mortal—knee-jerk pride and hunger for competition—will get you into hot water for four quarters. Of course, there is a level of football underlying even the most obscure high school confrontation. There are intramural college games, after-school games for distracted junior high students, and goofy, mixed-gender skirmishes at the company picnic. Grown-up buddies gather in groups of 6 or 10 to place orange cones, rope off sidelines, strap on flags, and knock the hell out of one another while the beer chills in the cooler. And then there is the bedrock of the entire pyramid: a vast, undisciplined army of children hopping around like hot popcorn kernels in practically every park, school, vacant lot, front yard, beach, and dead-end street in the country. Pick a sunny weekend afternoon in October, and there will be so many footballs in the air over America—punted footballs, thrown footballs, batted footballs, fumbled footballs—as to create a nationwide hazard for low-flying aircraft. In eastern Washington, two brothers, two sisters, and three cousins play three-on-three (plus a "permanent quarterback") on the family apple farm. In a Chicago public-housing project, kids who have never seen a farm chase down a half-inflated ball, wrapped in duct tape to stem previous puncture wounds. In a Dallas suburb, a white 9-year-old says he's Deion Sanders, and his Salvadoran friend says, okay, he'll be Troy Aikman. From coast to coast, they'll play until dark (or maybe one more touchdown after that) and recite their statistics (7 interceptions!) for their moms and dads at dinner. The thing about a pyramid is that our gaze is drawn skyward, to the jagged peak, but it's the base that supports the larger structure. The NFL is the pinnacle of the sport, a lure to everyone rising through the ranks, but the playground warriors who dream of making it there actually are the ones who hold the whole thing together. When people think of football, they picture Deion and Aikman, or maybe the Fighting Irish swarming the field to the tune of the Notre Dame fight song—and that's all right because the superstars and the super teams are effective ambassadors for the game. But what they really should think about is that boy playing in his driveway with a plastic football. His friends have gone home, but he isn't ready to retire for the night. So he enacts a one-man game, complete with trick plays, commentary, and pushing and shoving among rivals. He is the quarterback. He is the running back. He is the linebacker. He is football in America.

▲ Father and son work on their timing. East Rutherford, New Jersey.

◀ Flag-football acrobatics. Buffalo, New York.

Junior Bears on the march in Grant Park, Chicago, Illinois.

91

Which side goes on the front? Pembroke Pines, Florida.

A wet-and-wild first down.
Miami Beach, Florida.

THE EYES HAVE IT IN A BACKYARD SHOWDOWN. NAPERVILLE, ILLINOIS.

Pass routes on wheels. Santa Barbara, California.

Listen up! Here's the play. Key West, Florida.

64
HANTILL
64

Sandlot strategy session.
Centerville, Virginia.

FRIDAY-NIGHT SHOWDOWN. WARRENSVILLE, NORTH CAROLINA.

JUNEAU, ALASKA

Few things come easily on the Last Frontier. Certainly not football.

In Alaska, the high school football season starts earlier, ends sooner, and spans more miles per game than anywhere else in the United States. Weather dictates the season and then defines it.

The first league games are played in mid-August and the state champion is crowned in October. Even in that abbreviated season, the last few games usually are played in freezing temperatures on snow-covered fields.

In a vast state with few population centers, high school players often must travel hundreds of miles for a game.

Football in Alaska is demanding and at times downright harsh, but it also can be uncommonly beautiful. And there is no more spectacular

TRAINING DRILLS ON HILLSIDES CARVED OUT BY GLACIERS ARE ALL IN A DAY'S WORKOUT.

setting for a high school game than Anchorage Stadium with the Chugach Mountains rising above the light towers.

"There is a lot of sacrifice involved for the kids who play football here," says Dave Haynie, head coach at Juneau-Douglas High School. "The conditions are tough, the travel is tough, but kids stick with it because they love the game.

"For sheer desire, I'll stack our kids up against anybody. They know they have to work for everything. That's just how it is in Alaska, no matter what you do."

With its rugged glaciers and untamed wilderness, Alaska seems, in many ways, a world apart. Yet on an autumn night, when youngsters play football in Nikiski or Skyview and the band strikes up the fight song and pompons shake, it feels like any other town in America.

▲ When the Crimson Bears take the field, a spirited crowd greets them.

▶ Dave Haynie (pointing) has coached the team since its inception.

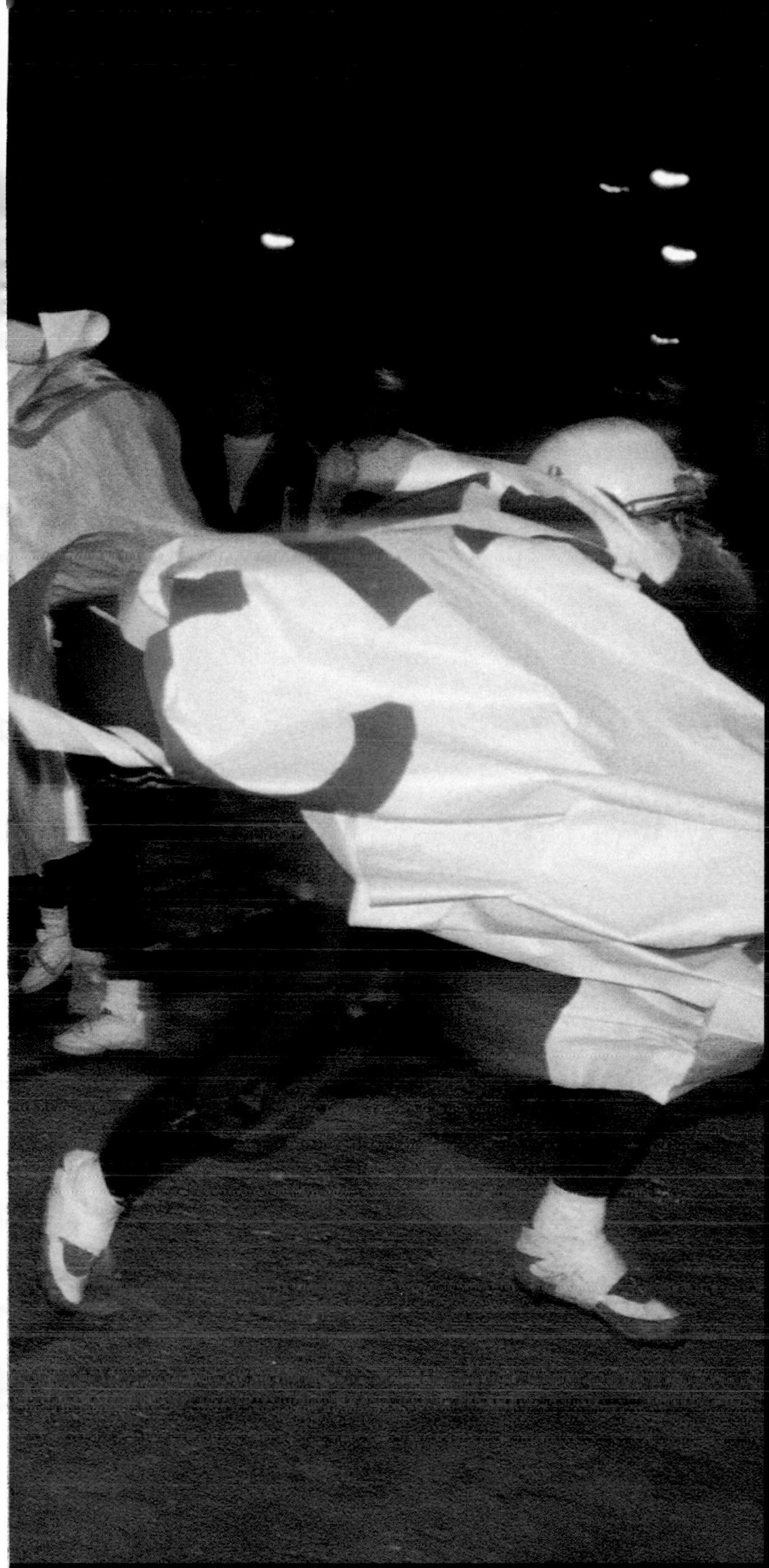

"The mere existence of high school football in Alaska," wrote Lew Freedman in the *Anchorage Daily News*, "is an affirmation that the forty-ninth state is one of the 50 states. If we have a Baskin-Robbins and McDonald's, then it is our inalienable right to have football, too."

The first high school football game in Alaska was played in 1951, eight years before Alaska was granted statehood. Anchorage High School, now West High, played a team of U.S. servicemen from Elmendorf Air Force Base.

The Anchorage players had little football experience. They wore makeshift uniforms with no facemasks or padding inside their helmets. They lost the game 24-12, but they kept working at it.

There was no television in Anchorage at the time. There wasn't much in the way of entertainment, so people rallied behind the football team. On the night before a game, there was a bonfire rally in the park, and several thousand people participated.

Word spread. Interest grew. The game took hold.

By 1952, Ketchikan High School had a team. Palmer High School followed suit.

By 1955, the Anchorage High program was far enough along that it wanted to test itself against outside competition. It brought in a team from Huntsville, Texas, for what was called the Santa Claus Bowl.

Huntsville won 12-6, but the Alaskans played the more experienced visitors on even terms most of the way.

Once Alaska became a state and the population grew, the game expanded. Today, there are 19 high schools, from Juneau to Fairbanks to the

▶ COMMITMENT IS A BYWORD FOR THE PLAYERS, WHO KNOW ABOUT OVERCOMING OBSTACLES.

Kenai Peninsula to Anchorage, playing varsity football.

There are three native Alaskans playing in the National Football League, including guard Mark Schlereth, who won a Super Bowl XXVI ring with the Washington Redskins in 1991. There are others playing at Division I colleges.

Alaska doesn't rival Texas or Florida for producing football players—its smaller talent pool and abbreviated season make that impossible—but the product on the field is quite polished and improving all the time.

Many Alaska schools now play their games on artificial turf. Rosters and coaching staffs are comparable in size to those of schools in other states. Most games are broadcast on the radio. The playoffs are televised across the state.

Alaskan football has come a long way since the Santa Claus Bowl. No program has come further, or endured more hardship along the way, than the one at Juneau-Douglas High School.

Juneau did not have a football team until 1990. Because of its remote location (south of Glacier Bay and 800 miles from Anchorage), it didn't

become a full member of the Cook Inlet Football Conference until 1995.

In Juneau, the school district provides financial support for other sports, but not for football. That means the program is supported entirely by the community, through ticket sales, car washes, bake sales, and raffles.

In 1995, the players, their families, and the Juneau Youth Football League raised more than $100,000 and still struggled to finish the seven-game season. It will be a struggle every year because of Juneau's geographic isolation from other CIFC schools.

Juneau, the state capital, is a beautiful city with majestic vistas, including the Mendenhall Glacier and Spaulding Meadows ski trail. At night, the city sparkles like a field of diamonds at the foot of the Chilkat Mountains. But Juneau is an island on the Gastineau Channel with more than half of its 3,000 square miles covered by ice or water. There are no roads leading on or off Juneau. There are only two ways to get there: by plane or boat.

In 1970, Juneau merged with Douglas, which is on an island across the channel, to form the largest city in the United States with an area of 3,100 square miles. There are only 26,000 residents in Juneau, and most of them work in the fishing, forestry, or tourism industries.

The Juneau-Douglas High School team flies to every away game, and when the Crimson Bears play at home, they pay the travel expenses of the visiting school. That was the deal Juneau-Douglas made to gain admission to the CIFC.

▲ A TEAM WITHOUT A DRESSING ROOM IS A TEAM THAT DRESSES WHEREVER IT CAN.

kids to come out and only eight showed up," Richie says. "Dave and I looked at each other and said, 'What do we do now?'

"We got them in a line for exercises and the next thing we knew, the police came and took away two kids for something they did the night before. Now we were down to six players.

"Dave asked me, 'What do you think?' I said, 'I think we'll have to be creative.' It was like any other new venture; it took time to get going. We were a little thin the first season but things grew steadily after that."

More than 50 candidates came out for the Juneau-Douglas team in 1995, and Haynie kept 40 on the varsity. The players reflect the mix of ethnic persuasions in Alaska: whites and blacks, as well as several youngsters from the Philippines and Tonga. One player, freshman Chad Bentz, was born without a right hand, but he plays fullback on offense and linebacker on defense. Each player paid for his own equipment ($200) and sold hundreds of dollars worth of raffle tickets and program advertising to cover the team's travel expenses.

The Crimson Bears played at the junior high school, but because the football program was not officially sanctioned by the school district, the coaches and players were not allowed to use the locker-room facilities.

The players dressed for practice in a hallway or in the parking lot. They were not allowed to shower at the school. One player, Josh Krieck, a 5-foot 10-inch, 390-pound defensive tackle, rode a city bus home every day after practice, still dressed in his grimy uniform.

Says Haynie: "No matter how crowded the bus was, Josh got a seat all to himself. It's not easy, but the kids handle it. I've never heard one complain."

"Bad as they are, the conditions do weed out the kids who are not as committed," says Richie,

THE SLATE-LIKE FIELD AT FLOYD DRYDEN STADIUM HAS RESULTED IN MORE THAN A FEW SCRAPED ELBOWS.

the defensive coordinator. "If a kid puts out the money and puts up with all the other stuff, like practicing in the rain and going home soaking wet, we know he must really love the game.

"You can't fake that kind of commitment. A kid either has it or he doesn't. The kids who play for us have it."

Whenever anyone talks about Juneau football, the conversation always comes back to one thing: the playing field at Floyd Dryden Stadium.

It is unlike any other playing surface in the state—perhaps in all of North America. There is not a blade of grass on the field. It is a slate gray mix of sand, rock, and gravel. The locals call it silt, the residue of glaciers which once dominated the island and have receded over time.

When rain falls, which it does through most of the football season in Juneau, the field is as hard and slippery as wet asphalt. When the field dries, it becomes abrasive.

There are rocks, pieces of glass, and bits of driftwood mixed in with the sand and clay. They work their way to the surface in rainstorms or when the field is dragged. The result is constant cuts and scrapes.

"We've had teams refuse to play us here," Haynie says. "A couple of schools from Oregon called and that was the first thing they said: 'We hear you have a dirt field.'

"I said, 'That's right.' They said, 'Well, we're not coming.' I said, 'Fine, we'll find somebody who will.'"

Before and after each practice, the Juneau

coaches and players walk the length of the field and clear debris. Each person's goal is to remove 20 foreign objects from the field.

Multiplied by 50 coaches and players, that's 1,000 pieces removed each day during the football season. But with each rain, more surface.

"You just do the best you can," Haynie says.

Visiting teams hate it, which makes the Juneau players love it. They pride themselves on being the hardest-hitting team in Alaska. That, coupled the harsh field conditions, give them a huge home-field advantage.

"It is intimidating," coach Mike Winters says. "I see other teams come in and look at our field. I know what those kids are thinking: 'I don't think I'm diving on any loose balls today.'

▲ PRACTICE SESSIONS ARE COLORFUL, WITH EACH PLAYER SUPPLYING HIS OWN JERSEY.

"Our kids have played on this since they were eight and nine years old. They don't even think twice about it. In fact, most of them like it."

When the Crimson Bears visited Chugiak, the game was played on a lush field of green grass. Many of the Juneau players complained it was too soft, that it slowed them down.

"It didn't even feel like the same game," said senior linebacker Todd Hansen. "You'd fall and you didn't even know it. I didn't get any scrapes or marks on my elbows.

"When you finish a game in Juneau, you know you've played football. That's the way we like it.'

Practice amid the sounds of the city in Bronx, New York.

Wind sprints mark the end of a workout at York High School in Elmhurst, Illinois.

A BROILING SUN FOR THE DALLAS COWBOYS' TRAINING CAMP IN AUSTIN, TEXAS...

…AND SHIVERS FOR GLENWOOD SPRINGS, COLORADO, HIGH SCHOOL.

The Arizona Cardinals begin a training-camp workout with pushups in Flagstaff, Arizona.

46

A young runner can't escape the shadows in Carbondale, Illinois.

In Moran, Texas, and towns like it, the game is played with six men to a side.

ODESSA & GUTHRIE, TEXAS

There is something unique about Texas high school football. Bathed in the Friday night lights, in towns such as Odessa, Plano, and Sweetwater, the games seem bigger, the emotions greater, the legends more enduring.

Other states, such as Florida, California, and Ohio, are just as rich in football talent. Pennsylvania has produced a line of great quarterbacks, from Johnny Unitas to Dan Marino. Mississippi can claim the NFL's all-time leading rusher (Walter Payton) and receiver (Jerry Rice).

But in Texas, football is more a religion than a game. On a typical autumn weekend, 4 million Texans fill high school stadiums from Port Arthur to Panther Creek, sharing in a ritual that goes back generations.

Every town, no matter how small, has its own boosters club, its own mothers club, its own identity tied to football. There may be very little to distinguish one rural town from another, but if the local high school team is undefeated, everyone across the state takes notice.

Season tickets for Temple High School are so precious, they are written into wills and contested in divorces. O.B. Graham, who owns the Texaco station in the central Texas town, did not miss a game, home or away, in 43 years.

When the Stephenville High School team travels, its bus is trailed by a caravan that stretches for miles. The cars are covered with streamers, and fans shake tin cans filled with ball bearings. The ear-splitting noise of the "Can Fans" is a Stephenville tradition. So is winning.

At Highland Park High School, where Doak Walker and Bobby Layne played in the 1940s, boosters hold candlelight vigils before big games.

Football advanced the cause of integration in Texas when the impact of black players such as Warren McVea, who led San Antonio's Brackenridge High to the state title in 1963, made other schools more willing to accept minorities.

Don Meredith, a native of Mount Vernon, Texas, believes football in general and high school football in particular symbolize what most Texans feel the state represents.

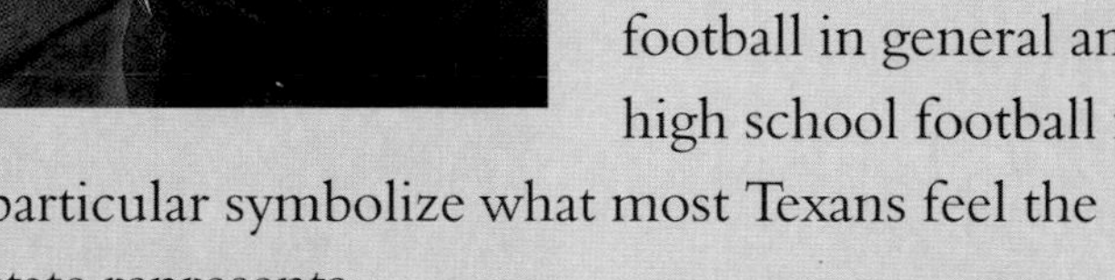

"Whether it's true or not, the image of Texas and of the settling of Texas is that it was done by rugged individuals who would physically stand their ground, who would physically settle an area," Meredith, the former Dallas Cowboys star, wrote in the book *The Rites of Fall*.

"Football, one town against another, became a great outlet for Texans, a way of saying this is what makes us best. But you don't realize any of

COACH HARVEY WELLMAN DIRECTS THE GUTHRIE HIGH SCHOOL JAGUARS.

this when you're growing up in Texas. I know I didn't. You just went out and played."

The names of football heroes such as Sammy Baugh, Kyle Rote, and Mean Joe Greene are as much a part of Texas folklore as Sam Houston and Stephen Austin. Certain players will be linked forever with their hometowns, such as Earl Campbell in Tyler and Bill Bradley in Palestine.

For a boy in Texas, football is a birthright. It is something he grows into, like his brother's varsity jacket. From the time he is old enough to walk, he is drawn to the glow of the stadium lights and the spectacle of a marching band playing "The Eyes of Texas" on a crisp October night.

"Growing up in a town like Abilene, those games were the biggest event of the week," says Jack Mildren, one of the top high school quarterbacks in Texas history, later an All-America at Oklahoma.

"Everyone would go—from little kids to senior citizens. As kids, we'd have our own games going on behind the end zone. Abilene would be winning by forty points, and we'd be there, playing

▲ FANS JAM THE STANDS AND THE TOWN COMES TO A STANDSTILL WHEN ODESSA FACES PERMIAN.

among ourselves, listening to the crowd cheer.

"We'd pretend the cheers were for us. All we ever thought about was someday being on the field, wearing one of those uniforms and playing for real. It made me tingle just thinking about it.

"In Texas, that was how life was supposed to be."

Nowhere in the state is that feeling stronger than Odessa, where the Panthers of Permian High School play in a $5.6 million stadium with artificial turf and a seating capacity of 19,032. On game night, every seat is filled and there are more fans jamming the aisles and standing along the fence. And against crosstown rival Odessa High School in the season's big game, fans are packed along the fence.

Odessa is a working-class town, 350 miles west of Dallas and 300 miles east of El Paso, squarely in the middle of West Texas oil country and not close to much else. Just follow Highway 80 to the last row of oil derricks and turn left. You will see the sign:

"Home of the Permian Panthers, State Champions Football [Class] AAAAA, 1965, '72, '80, '84."

All over Odessa there are posters and bumper stickers with the word: "*Mojo*." That is the Permian battle cry—what the fans chant during games and what the coaches shout at players when they are gasping for breath as practice winds down.

Mojo. It is Permian football—the tradition, the pride, the mission—all wrapped up in one word. *Mojo*. It is a powerful force that turns teenage boys of modest ability into champions.

The 1980 Permian team was typical: undersized, with a line that averaged 180 pounds, and with only one starter (tackle Roy Dunn) who would play at the college level. Yet that team won the state title.

In the championship game, Permian faced a Port Arthur Jefferson team considered one of the best in Texas schoolboy history. A dozen players from that team went to Division I colleges on football scholarships. Five played at the University of Texas.

But playing before a capacity crowd at Texas Stadium, the bigger and faster Port Arthur team lost 28-19 to Permian. Jefferson led 19-7 at halftime, but Permian fought back with three unanswered touchdowns to score the shocking upset.

Port Arthur quarterback Todd Dodge says the game was decided not by strategy, but by the sheer will of the Permian players. "We'd block 'em and they'd roll over and get up, and we'd block 'em and they'd roll over and get up, and we'd block 'em and they'd roll over and get up again," Dodge says.

That is the essence of *Mojo*.

Britt Hager was in the stands that night, watching his older brother Kevin play guard for Permian.

Three years later, Britt was an All-America fullback and linebacker at Permian. Britt Hager is one of the few Permian players to make the jump to big-time college football. He was a standout linebacker at Texas and in 1989 was drafted by the Philadelphia Eagles. He played six seasons with the Eagles before signing with the Denver Broncos in 1995.

Prior to Hager, only one Permian player had made it to the pros: Daryl Hunt, a linebacker, spent six seasons with Houston. It seems like a contradiction: a high school program that ranks among the most successful in Texas, yet turns out few players able to compete at higher levels.

To understand it, Hager says, you have to be part of the Permian family.

"It's tradition, it's hard work, it's all the things other teams talk about, but don't really practice," Hager says. "At Permian, that's what makes the difference. It's real. You grow up with it.

"When you're a third grader in Odessa, you don't think about what college you want to play

for, or what pro team you want to play for. All you think is, 'I want to play for Permian.' You'll do whatever it takes to wear that black-and-white jersey."

The football teams at the elementary schools, which provide the feeder system for Permian, run the Permian offensive and defensive systems. It's the same with the junior high schools. So when a player reaches the tenth grade, he knows the system by heart.

Each year, the coaches weed out the 100 or so varsity candidates by putting them through a pre-season boot camp that includes workouts in a gym heated to 100 degrees and wind sprints while shouldering a tire.

"You keep going until you throw up," Hager says. "Then you go some more."

The chosen few who make the team are reminded they are playing not just for themselves; they are playing for the teams that went before, for the boosters who helped pay for the stadium and the charter flights to the state playoffs, for all the people in Odessa who look to them as a source of pride.

Each player is assigned a Pepette, a girl from the senior class who bakes him cakes, makes posters with his name for pep rallies, and wears

his number to the games. Britt Hager wound up marrying his Pepette, Bridgette, who also was the homecoming queen.

"What happens is you realize you're part of something that's a whole lot bigger than yourself," Hager says. "You walk onto that field, look around, and you say, 'I can't let these people down.'

"My junior year, I tore cartilage in my hip. I took shots, pain killers, to keep playing. I didn't tell my parents because I was afraid they'd make me sit out. I wound up with an infection that required surgery after the season.

"Some people may say it was the pressure to win that made me play hurt. But, really, I did it for my teammates. I felt like I owed it to them. I knew they'd do the same for me. That was the kind of feeling we had for each other.

"That's how Permian wins with teams that are outweighed by forty pounds a man. Guys play bigger than they are, better than they are, because they don't want to let down the rest of the team, their family, the fans, everybody."

There is another brand of football played in Texas, smaller in scale, but comparable in feeling. It is six-man football, played at high schools with an enrollment of 85 or fewer students.

There are about 90 such schools in Texas, most located in the western part of the state where cattle ranches sprawl for miles and each town consists of a post office, a church, and little else.

The six-man game was invented in 1934 by a coach in Nebraska, Stephen Epler. He thought it was unfair that youngsters could be denied football just because they went to a school where there were not enough boys to field an 11-man team.

Epler designed a scaled-down version of the game in which the offense had a center, two ends, and three backs. The field is 80 yards long and 40 yards wide. Some rules are different (15 yards for a first down) and scoring is modified (four points for a field goal).

The game caught on and spread to other states. In Texas, a future NFL star, Jack Pardee, dominated the six-man league while playing for Christoval High School. Pardee scored 356 points in his senior season.

"We were a tiny school: eight in our senior class, four boys and four girls," Pardee says. "But people loved watching our games. There were only 500 people in the town, but we had crowds of 1,500 at some games. They came from miles away.

"It was a fun game to play and to watch. There

was a lot of open field and the ball was in the air on every play. It was like playing basketball, only with blocking and tackling."

All six players are eligible to catch a pass in six-man football. The quarterback—or whomever takes the snap from center—cannot cross the line of scrimmage with the ball unless he hands off to

another player and then receives it back.

There are laterals on almost every play and lots of razzle-dazzle. It is not unusual for a center to catch a touchdown pass, or throw one to the quarterback. Teams often combine to score more than 100 points in a game.

There is sweet innocence to a six-man game played against the backdrop of a small Texas town. The halftime show often includes one or two players, in full football uniform, including pads, marching with the school band. The star halfback may celebrate a victory by helping his Mom clean the snack bar.

In towns such as Guthrie (population 100),

The rites of autumn: Fans feast before 'Bama meets Auburn.

WISCONSIN CHEERLEADERS WARM UP THE CROWD. MADISON, WISCONSIN.

Auburn's War Eagle sizes up its prey. Auburn, Alabama.

VOLS

Tennessee at Kentucky: Make way for the Vols. Lexington, Kentucky.

THE NOTRE DAME MASCOT GETS A WEE BIT WOUND UP WHEN THE OPPONENT IS USC.

SOUTH BEND, INDIANA

College football rivalries take shape in many ways. Some are about state bragging rights—Auburn vs. Alabama, Florida vs. Florida State. Others grow out of years of conference play—Michigan vs. Ohio State, Oklahoma vs. Nebraska. Army-Navy is a natural rivalry, built on spit and polish and trimmed in gold braid. The Harvard-Yale series has a heritage that dates back to 1875 and includes some of college football's greatest names, from Amos Alonzo Stagg to Calvin Hill.

What makes the Notre Dame-Southern California rivalry unique is that the Irish and the Trojans would not appear to have much reason to face off. Theirs is not a border war, because the campuses are three time zones apart. There are no conference standings at stake because Notre Dame competes as an independent in football.

Notre Dame, the small Catholic school in Indiana, and USC, the big private school in Los Angeles, were drawn together by the gravitational pull of their football excellence. Notre Dame and USC so dominated the college game—they have produced a combined 11 Heisman Trophy winners and 19 national championships—that there was no way they could avoid each other. They had to meet, if only to sort out their places in history.

Starting in 1926 with Knute Rockne and continuing for generations, with players such as Joe Montana and Anthony Davis, the rivalry has brought out the best in each school. They have met 10 times when one school was ranked number one. In most cases, the other was not far behind.

Former Notre Dame quarterback Joe Theismann, who passed for a school-record 526 yards in a loss to USC in 1970, says, "We were good and we knew it. Southern Cal was good and they knew it. When we played, it was like two gunfighters meeting in the center of town. You wanted to settle it: Who's the best? Those are the games you love to play in."

Rod Sherman, a receiver for USC from 1964 through 1966, says "I liked reading the program before the game, looking at the Notre Dame roster. They had players from every state, the best athletes in the country. I'd look at that, my heart would start pounding, and I'd think: 'Man, this is the BIG time.'"

From the beginning, it was a rivalry that stirred the emotions. In 1929, Rockne was bedridden with blood clots in his legs, but he insisted on coaching against USC from a wheelchair. The Irish won 13-12 before an overflow crowd of 112,912 at Chicago's Soldier Field.

▲ ARMS UPRAISED, "TOUCHDOWN JESUS" OVERLOOKS NOTRE DAME STADIUM.

Two years later, following Rockne's death in a plane crash, the Trojans snapped Notre Dame's 26-game unbeaten streak with a 16-14 upset in South Bend, Indiana. A crowd of 300,000 turned out to greet the USC team when it returned to Los Angeles. A movie of the game broke attendance records in theaters from coast to coast.

Perhaps the most famous figure in the series is Anthony Davis, the USC tailback who played from 1972-74. He holds the series record for most points (68) and most touchdowns (11). Davis scored 6 touchdowns (2 on kickoff returns) in the 1972 game, which the Trojans won 45-23. Two years later, he scored four times, highlighted by a 100-yard kickoff return, to lead USC back from a 24-0 deficit to a 55-24 victory. It was one of the greatest comebacks in college football history.

After the latter game, Davis recalls, a woman in a black dress approached him and waved a small crucifix in his face and said, "No one has ever done what you've done to Notre Dame. You

EMOTIONS ARE HIGH AND THE HITS ARE HARD WHEN THE IRISH AND TROJANS COLLIDE.

Dame. When I look at it that way, I really owe those guys."

Notre Dame coach Lou Holtz has said he considers USC the biggest opponent on the schedule each year, even though games against Florida State, Michigan, and Miami occasionally have had a greater bearing on national rankings.

The Trojans slipped in the early 1990s and Notre Dame took control of the series, building an unbeaten streak that reached 13 games in 1995. But Holtz is a traditionalist who appreciates the history of college football. He knows the USC rivalry is, like George Gipp and the Golden Dome, an essential part of Notre Dame lore.

Each year, Holtz gives a one-hour lecture about the rivalry to all first-year players. The week of the game, Holtz gives the newcomers a written test. Any player who fails the test is not allowed to dress for the game.

"It is coach's way of making the point that this isn't just another game," says fullback Mark Edwards, who scored 3 touchdowns in Notre Dame's 38-10 victory over USC in 1995. "At first, it seems silly, approaching a game like it's a history course. But then you see what he is driving at. The more he talks and you hear about the games and some of the unbelievable things that happened, you think: 'Wow, now I'm a part of

must be the devil." Then she disappeared into the crowd.

"I still get magazine covers in the mail, people wanting my autograph twenty years later," Davis says. "I could've played fifteen seasons in the NFL and been most valuable player in five Super Bowls and I'd still be remembered for those three games. All because it was against Notre

THE IRISH BOOSTER CLUB KICKS OFF THE WEEKEND WITH A SPIRITED FRIDAY LUNCHEON.

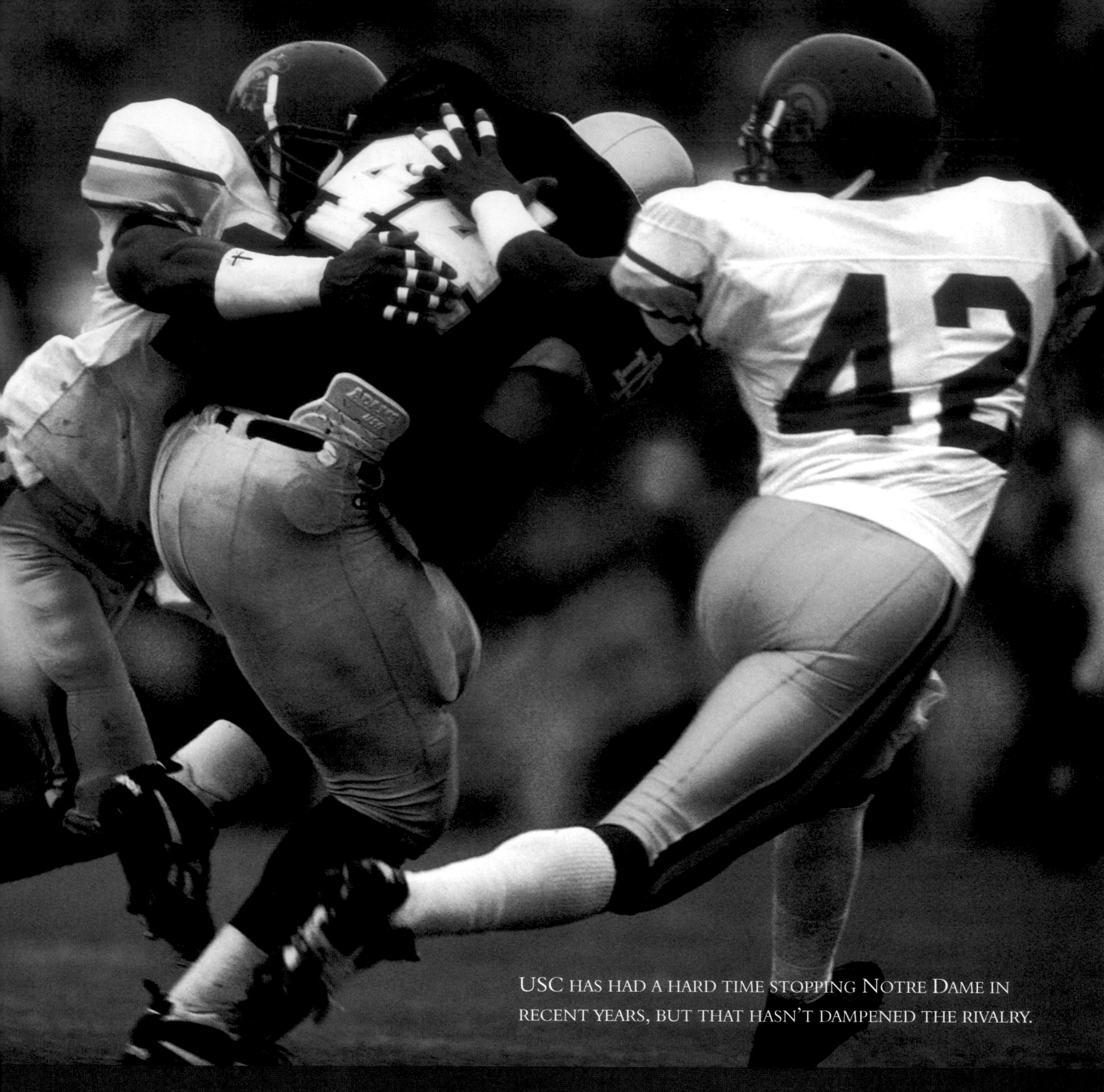

USC HAS HAD A HARD TIME STOPPING NOTRE DAME IN RECENT YEARS, BUT THAT HASN'T DAMPENED THE RIVALRY.

this.' It's like a pep talk and history course rolled into one. I took notes and everything."

To date, no player has failed the test and, under Holtz, the Irish never have lost to USC (9-0-1).

Notre Dame and USC rank first and seventh respectively in all-time winning percentage among Division I-A football programs. Between them, the schools have produced more than 291 All-America players and sent 63 coaches and players to the College Football Hall of Fame. Five of the 12 highest-rated college football telecasts are Notre Dame-USC games. The two schools drew the largest crowd ever to see a football game at the Los Angeles Memorial Coliseum —104,953 in 1947. Notre Dame leads the series with 39 victories but has lost more games to USC (23) than to any other school. There have been 5 ties in the series.

Each school has a proud tradition, a loyal alumni, and a great fight song. Each team still plays on its landmark field—Notre Dame Stadium in South Bend, the Coliseum in Los Angeles—giving the games a timeless quality that is rare in this era of domed stadiums and artificial turf.

"Playing in those games, it just seemed like that's the way college football should be," says Jim Lynch, who captained the 1966 Notre Dame team that won a national championship. "I remember warming up in the Coliseum and seeing the Southern Cal band come out, all those pretty girls, all those Trojan costumes, hundreds of them. I looked at the [USC] team, which was headed to the Rose Bowl. It was one of those moments where it just hits you—how lucky you are to be there."

Compared to the setting in Los Angeles, the games in South Bend usually are gray and cold.

In 1995, when Notre Dame and USC met for the fiftieth consecutive season, a chilling rain fell most of the day. But the atmosphere at Notre Dame on a football weekend is such that weather hardly matters. If the temperature happens to be cold enough to raise a few goosebumps on the USC sidelines, no one in the home crowd is going to feel too bad.

On a classic football Saturday in South Bend, the sun glints off the Golden Dome. But the magic of the setting goes well beyond that. Notre Dame's mystique lies in its rich football heritage. On game day, the faithful wrap that century of tradition around themselves as if it were a blue-and-gold shawl. On campus, students grill hot dogs and hamburgers while the glee club sings songs such as "Hike, Notre Dame" and "Irish Backs [Go Rolling By]." Bagpipers stroll among the tailgaters while the voice of Rockne, in a recorded pep talk, echoes unmistakably from a dormitory window.

The school has many religious landmarks, the most famous of which have been popularized in football terms. There is Touchdown Jesus, the 10-story Mosaic of Christ, arms upraised, which overlooks the football stadium from the west. There is a bronze statue of Moses, also facing the stadium, his index finger thrust proudly to the sky. The Irish, he seems to be indicating, are number one. A short distance away, there is a statue of the Reverend William Corby, a former Notre Dame president, right hand raised, bestowing a blessing on the Irish brigade before the Battle of Gettysburg. That part of the story is almost forgotten. Today, he is better known as "Fair Catch" Corby, patron saint of reluctant punt returners.

Religion and football always have been linked at Notre Dame. When Michael and John Shea wrote the now-famous "Notre Dame Victory March" in 1908, they played it first on the pipe organ in the chapel. It is a game-day tradition for the Notre Dame players and coaches to attend Mass together in the chapel and then walk across

▶ TIME AND TIME AGAIN, OPPORTUNITY ELUDED THE TROJANS' GRASP.

campus, through a column of cheering fans, to the stadium.

On one wall of the Notre Dame locker room, beneath a crucifix, is a plaque with the last words uttered by a dying George Gipp, the school's All-America halfback, to Rockne in 1920: "Tell them to go in there with all they've got and win just one for the Gipper." On another wall, there are two posters in blue and gold that list the names of Notre Dame's many All-Americas, from Gipp through Paul Hornung to Rocket Ismail.

As the players head for the field, they walk down a staircase dominated by a large sign. It lists the 11 national championship seasons and reads: "Notre Dame Tradition, Play Like a

A CONCERT ON THE STEPS OF THE GOLDEN DOME HAS BECOME A GAME-DAY CUSTOM.

Champion Today." Each player touches the sign on his way to the field.

In 1995, USC coach John Robinson tried to combat the Notre Dame tradition by importing some tradition of his own. He invited one of his former All-Americas, Anthony Muñoz, to join the team in South Bend. The Trojans had not beaten Notre Dame since 1982. Robinson thought a pep talk from Muñoz, who starred on USC's last unbeaten team in 1979, might give the players a lift. The 1979 team crushed the Irish in South Bend 42-23.

"We have a rivalry with UCLA, but it isn't as intense as the rivalry with Notre Dame," says Muñoz, an offensive tackle who later starred for the Cincinnati Bengals. "With UCLA, we knew

USC
42
ADAMS

◀ THE RIVALRY, WHICH BEGAN IN 1926, GENERATES A RENEWED INTENSITY EACH YEAR.

most of the players. We'd see them around town. They were pretty much like us. But with Notre Dame, it was like a hate thing. They just seem to market themselves as *the team*. All you ever heard about was Rockne and the Gipper and the Four Horsemen. We got tired of it. We resented it because we felt we had a great tradition, too. We saw Notre Dame as a program that walked around with its nose in the air. We wanted to knock them back down to earth."

Muñoz's first trip to South Bend was the 1977 game, when the Irish pulled a famous jersey switch on the Trojans. Coach Dan Devine surprised the Notre Dame team by issuing kelly green jerseys in the locker room just minutes before kickoff. Notre Dame, which warmed up in its traditional blue jerseys, had not worn green in a game since 1963. No one knew Devine had smuggled the new shirts into the stadium until that moment. The players went bonkers when they saw them, and the crowd exploded when the surging mass of green poured out of the

▲ JOHN ROBINSON (CENTER) KNOWS HOW HARD IT IS TO BEAT NOTRE DAME AT SOUTH BEND.

▶ WHEN IRISH EYES ARE SMILING, THE ONLY COLOR THEY CAN SEE IS GREEN.

tunnel. The Trojans, who had lost only once to Notre Dame in the previous 10 years and were ranked fifth in the polls to Notre Dame's eleventh, never had a chance that day. The inspired Irish routed USC 49-19, as Montana passed for 2 touchdowns and ran for 2 more.

Los Angeles Times columnist Jim Murray described the Notre Dame team as "Forty-five players with the grace of God purring in their hearts and the colors of Paddy gracing their shoulders."

"I thought I was seeing things when they came out in those jerseys," Muñoz says. "We were all fired up and, bam, that took the emotion right out of our team. When we went back to South Bend two years later, you'd better believe we had revenge on our minds."

The Trojans got their revenge in 1979 as Charles White, the eventual Heisman Trophy winner, carried 44 times (a record for Notre Dame opponents) for 261 yards. Muñoz had to miss playing in the game because of a knee injury, but watched from the sideline.

When Muñoz went back to South Bend in 1995, he was accompanied by his 15-year-old son, Michael. The younger Muñoz, who already is as big as an NFL lineman, stunned his father a few years earlier by announcing he wanted to attend Notre Dame. Michael was born and raised in Cincinnati, a Notre Dame stronghold.

Anthony Muñoz hoped that if his son spent the weekend with the USC players and stood on their side of the field during the game, he would convert. But Michael spent one afternoon in the bookstore, buying Notre Dame hats and T-shirts. Then the Irish handed the Trojans their first loss of the season.

"It was a disappointing game because I felt this was the year we would break the [winless] streak against Notre Dame," Muñoz says. "We were six-and-oh coming into the game, Notre Dame had not played that well, and I really felt we had the better team. When I talked to the players the night before the game, I told them they couldn't take anything for granted. I said 'This is Notre Dame, and you're playing in their house. They will fight you to the death.' That's the nature of that team and the nature of the rivalry.

"Watching the game, I could see the USC players were bigger and stronger but the Notre Dame players just outhit them. It was intense."

The Notre Dame players were inspired by

comments attributed to USC receiver Keyshawn Johnson that suggested the Irish were overrated and not worth national television exposure every week. Johnson, an All-America, insists he never said those things, but Holtz tossed the quotes on the bonfire just the same.

"We know how other schools feel about us," Notre Dame's Mark Edwards says. "We know there is a lot of jealousy out there. It is something we hear all the time. But anyone who runs down this program doesn't know what he's talking about. We were ready for [Johnson], that's for sure. I still think Southern Cal is our number-one rivalry.

"Just because we haven't lost to them in a long time doesn't take away the tradition; it just puts a different spin on it. Those guys probably want to win more now than they ever did. And we sure don't want to lose because we don't want to have to face the guys who played here the last ten years and explain why we couldn't keep the streak going."

MAXPRO
MAXPRO
MAXPRO

facemask. Chances are, you follow the ball. It's what we have been programmed to do. But you could just as easily watch the center every play, and you'd end up with a unique view of the game—a hidden drama usually revealed only to his mother and his position coach. Foreign fans, though captivated by the spectacle of football, often are annoyed by the huddles between every play. They are frustrated by the pauses in the running action, but those of us who have grown up with the game need the respite as much as the players do. It's like moving a piano: you rest...you heave and grunt with all your might... you rest...you heave and grunt... Between huddles there is bedlam. Elbows fly, eyes dart, knees churn, shoulders dip, and entire bodies hurtle through the air. Towels, mouthpieces, shoes, and even headgear wind up strewn about the turf. Is this the aftermath of a routine draw to the fullback, or a tornado in a sporting goods store? The color is dizzying. The helmets sparkle like jewels under a bright sun or the beams of stadium lights. The jerseys practically bleed color. It might be the Philadelphia Eagles' green or Navy's blue. The shirts might say Barron's Bail Bonds or nothing at all, not even a number. In any case, the hues of football make it nearly impossible to turn your head and look away. There is noise, too. You get a few localized sounds on television, from whatever direction the network sound mike happens to be aimed. Up close, though, it's tumult. The players bark, roar, and cry out in agony. The coaches shout, "Pass! Pass! Pass!" The 44 feet of 22 athletes create an elephantine din as they are put in motion. And the collision of pads sounds like a demolition derby involving plastic Chevies. Sometimes you swear you can hear it with the television muted. At its best, football looks like battlefield ballet, like a weird scene that didn't make the final cut of *Apocalypse Now*. A high school quarterback bootlegs and finds himself in a one-on-one sprint against the "rover," ending with a dive to the padded orange marker. A University of Tennessee sophomore arrives at the same moment as a pass over the middle, drilling the intended receiver into three seconds of serenity followed by three days of hurt. Seventeen men crowd the 1-yard line as if someone is about to toss a gold brick down the line. They collide at the first twitch, turning the neutral zone into mass wreckage. And then there is the form of Marshall Faulk, aloft, 200 pounds (220 including equipment) defying gravity on a solo flight to the end zone. Most of us could not leap that far from a diving board, but we don't resent his ability. Rather, we're happy for the opportunity to witness such a marvel. Our only complaint is that it happens just once a week.

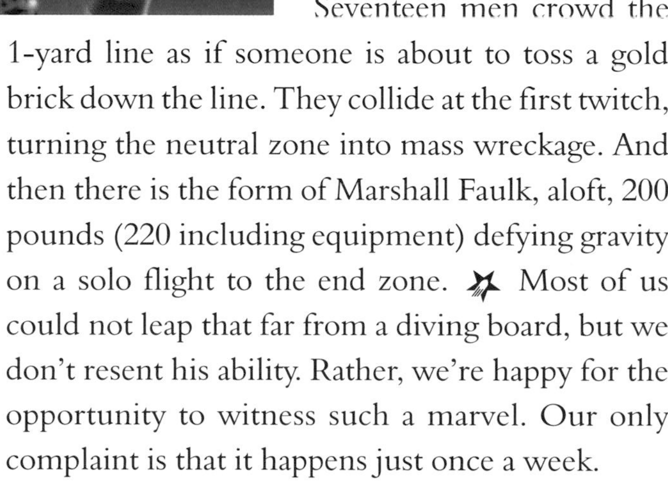

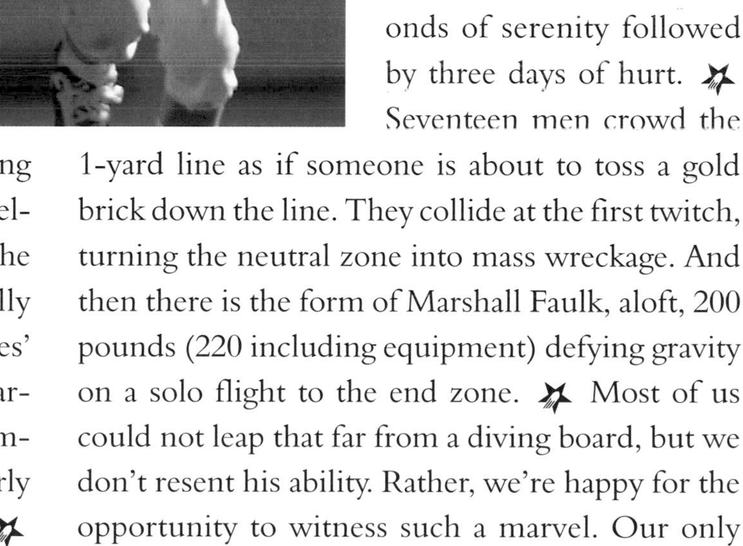

▲ A SHARK ATTACKS DURING THIRD-GRADE FLAG FOOTBALL. GARLAND, TEXAS.

◀ MUD IN YOUR EYE: NORTH PENN HIGH SCHOOL ON DEFENSE. LANSDALE, PENNSYLVANIA.

FRANCIS
33

A WIDE-OPEN FIELD AND RACE TO THE END ZONE. SAN FRANCISCO, CALIFORNIA.

Gators
79
NIKE

A leak in the pass protection: Florida vs. Florida State. Gainesville, Florida.

A HARD DAY ON SPECIAL TEAMS: THE RAMS' TODD KINCHEN TAKES A SPILL. ST. LOUIS, MISSOURI.

Touchdown, Tennessee!
Peyton Manning reaches
the end zone at Kentucky.

RAIDERS
Riddell
11

Vince Evans of the Raiders searches for an escape. Oakland, California.

Man vs. the elements. Williamstown, Massachusetts.

GRATERFORD, PENNSYLVANIA

The walls around the State Correctional Institution in Graterford, Pennsylvania, are thirty feet high. Alan Presbury has been staring at them since 1974 when he was sentenced to life imprisonment for murder.

The only time Presbury is not aware of the walls, the only time he feels free, is when he is on the football field.

"I'm not locked up out there," Presbury says. "It's like I'm somewhere else. When you get the ball, you feel like you can run forever."

As a quarterback, Presbury led the Graterford team in the Delaware Valley Semipro Conference until 1985 when it was expelled after one of its games ended in a brawl. The prison discontinued the semipro team but started an intramural rough-touch program, which now has six teams and more than 100 players. Presbury is the commissioner and head referee.

"When they took away the old program, I wasn't right for two months," Presbury says. "I moped around my cell. I didn't want to do anything. That team was the biggest thing we had.

"But the new league gave us something to grab on to. If it wasn't for sports, I would've gave up long ago. Sports keep me in a positive frame of mind. I get up in the morning and I have something to look forward to."

There are 10 sports available to the inmates in Graterford, a maximum-security facility located 30 miles north of Philadelphia. Football and boxing are the most popular, inmates say, because they offer the best emotional release.

"There is a lot of frustration and anger here," says Tom Gaskins, who oversees the prison recreation program. "Sports gives the inmates a chance to get rid of that anger.

"We're all competitive. It's no different here. I hear inmates saying, 'Our team is the best, we're gonna do it this year.' When they win, it's a big deal. It's bragging rights."

The league is run entirely by the inmates, beginning each fall when the team captains meet to draft their players for the season.

The inmates set up the rules, coach the teams, and even officiate the games. The season begins in October and continues until March when the two teams with the best records meet for the championship.

The games are highly competitive, but almost always under control. That is because the players know they can be banned from the league and lose their recreation privileges if they cause a disturbance.

"[The inmates] run things even stricter than the staff would because we don't want a few

▲ ALAN PRESBURY (ABOVE), SERVING A LIFE TERM, IS THE COMMISSIONER AND HEAD REFEREE.

THE GAMES PROVIDE A MUCH-NEEDED EMOTIONAL RELEASE.

troublemakers messing things up for the rest of us," Presbury says. "If something happened, like a fight in a game, the prison might shut down the program and we'd all lose. We had it happen with the semipro team so now we all depend on each other and keep everyone in line."

Games are played on weekends in the prison yard. Guards circle the dirt field and watch from the towers above. Dozens of inmates stand along the sidelines, cheering the action.

On Sundays, when the rough-touch games end, most of the 5,000 prisoners return to the cell block and watch NFL games on television. Some inmates have their own sets. The others watch the community television in the hall.

"Football is one thing that brings the prison population together," Gaskins says. "That's all they do on weekends—play football and watch football. When the games are on, everything else stops."

"Most of the guys are from the Philadelphia area so they're Eagles fans," Presbury says.

▲ THE PRISON WALLS ARE NEARLY FORGOTTEN WHEN A GAME IS GOING ON.

"When the Eagles are on TV and something happens, like a long run or an interception, there's all this yelling. You can be anywhere in the building and you hear the noise. You'll know exactly what it is."

Once a year, usually on Christmas Day, the inmates have an all-star game with the best players from the league forming two teams. For one game, they play tackle football, without helmets or pads.

"Some guys look at it and say, 'No thanks, that's too rough for me,'" Gaskins says. "But most guys love it. It's like their Christmas present. They get to play all out. They get some bumps and bruises, but it's usually not much more than that.

"It's a real competitive thing for these guys. We have a number of inmates who were good athletes in high school, who might've been good

"WHEN THEY WIN, IT'S A BIG DEAL," THE PROGRAM'S DIRECTOR SAYS. "IT'S BRAGGING RIGHTS."

enough to play in college or even at the next level, but they made a mistake and wound up here.

"For them, playing in these games is one way of staying in touch with that other part of their lives. A guy scores a touchdown here, he smiles just as wide as a guy playing anywhere else."

HAPPINESS MEANS THE JUNIOR VARSITY CHAMPIONSHIP FOR THE EAST ORIENTAL PEEWEES.

AKRON, OHIO

The ritual was familiar to every youngster who played organized football in Akron, Ohio: equipment inspection, by a small, gruff man.

Only when Gary Steffee finished checking the helmet, the chin strap, the shoulder pads, the hip pads, everything, including the athletic supporter, was a peewee player allowed on the field.

"I was called Little Caesar because I was so strict," says Steffee, who founded the Parent Peewee Football Association in Akron. "Every team would line up and I'd inspect each player, one at a time.

"I made sure their pads were okay and their shoes were okay. Sometimes I'd find kids who had stuff on backwards or forgot it altogether. One kid showed up without shoulder pads. He said, 'I don't need 'em. I'm mean.' I told him to get the pads or he didn't play.

"I've gotten older and softer, but I still won't let kids play wearing jewelry. Earrings, chains, all that stuff has to come off. Everything I do is for the kids' protection."

Peewee football was Steffee's life from the time he started the Akron league in 1964 until 1995 when he retired as commissioner. He worked 12 months a year on the program, sharing the

▶ FOUNDER GARY STEFFEE (LEFT) HAS BEEN SYNONYMOUS WITH THE LEAGUE SINCE 1964.

administrative duties with his wife Dorothy.

The Steffees ordered the equipment, screened the coaches, hired the officials, and enrolled the players, ages 8 to 13. Gary and Dorothy ran the whole program from their home. Every player's application, dating back to the first year, still can be found on file in their basement.

"Gary ran the league with one idea in mind: 'Do what's best for the kids,'" says Tim Bryan, who played in the league for five years and came back to coach after college. "He is unwavering in his principles. For thirty years, he made every decision and he made some people angry. But a number of the people who had disputes with Gary now are his best friends because they understand he was acting on the kids' behalf.

"He's the most selfless man I've ever met. Every summer he opened up his house so hundreds of kids could come in and get weighed on the official scale—his scale. How many people do you know who would do that?"

Steffee worked the night shift at the Firestone plant for more than 30 years. He organized the football league to give area youngsters something to do after school. He never imagined it would grow to include teams from more than 20 districts. One of the players, Don Buckey, even went on to earn a roster spot with the New York Jets.

"I felt if I could keep a few kids off the streets, it would be worth it," Steffee says. "Teach them a little respect, give them a little discipline, improve their physical fitness. All of that is good for kids.

"It turned out to be a bigger program than I expected. It became like a full-time job. My wife and I didn't take a vacation for years because there was so much to do. But it was worth it.

"Quite a few of the kids went on to play college football. Some wound up at big schools, like Ohio State and Notre Dame. When you see that,

◄ Coach Tim Fowler exhorts the West Griffins in the Varsity title game.
▼ Dorothy has always been at Gary's side.

GRIFFINS
7

you feel like you did something good."

Over the years, the peewee program mirrored the city of Akron, flourishing in the 1970s and declining in the 1980s as factories closed and unemployment hit record highs.

Steffee kept the league going because he saw the value in bringing together youngsters from different backgrounds. The program has players and coaches from affluent areas competing alongside players and coaches from the housing projects on Akron's south side.

"For some of the younger kids, this is their first real contact with someone who's a different color," Steffee says. "Being on a team brings them together. You can say, 'See, that boy's the same as you.' Kids learn so much that way.

"Teaching them the game, that's another story. We get kids who don't know their right from their left. Give 'em a play and they forget it by the time they reach the huddle. I tell the coaches, 'Teach 'em as much as you can, but make sure they have fun. That's the important part.'"

The league also has cheerleaders, and they, too, came under Steffee's authority. Uniforms had to be worn in an acceptable fashion and all cheers were subject to his approval.

Steffee retired as commissioner so that he and Dorothy could have more time for themselves. Dorothy participated in interviewing each coaching applicant.

Dorothy did not hesitate to reject someone if she felt he was more concerned with winning than teaching kids how to play.

"We don't need people on ego trips," she says. "Most of our coaches have the right idea. They're in it for the kids. The others, we weed out."

Gary Steffee was a strict administrator. He suspended players who talked back to coaches and referees. He dismissed any coach who cursed or smoked on the field. He once fired a referee for chewing tobacco during a game.

"The first time he spit, I told him to pack up his gear and leave," Steffe says. "I didn't want the kids putting their hands down in that mess.

"A newspaper got ahold of the story and made a big deal of it, but I'd do it again. Nobody spits on my field."

Gallaudet University, the only accredited liberal arts college for deaf students, has a football tradition that dates back more than 100 years.

The huddle, which now is as much a part of the game as the forward pass, originated at Gallaudet. Paul Hubbard, the school's quarterback from 1892 to 1895, recognized the problem of using sign language to call plays. Done in the open, hand signs were easily stolen by the opposition.

Hubbard moved the team several yards off the ball and positioned the players so their backs were to the line of scrimmage. That allowed the

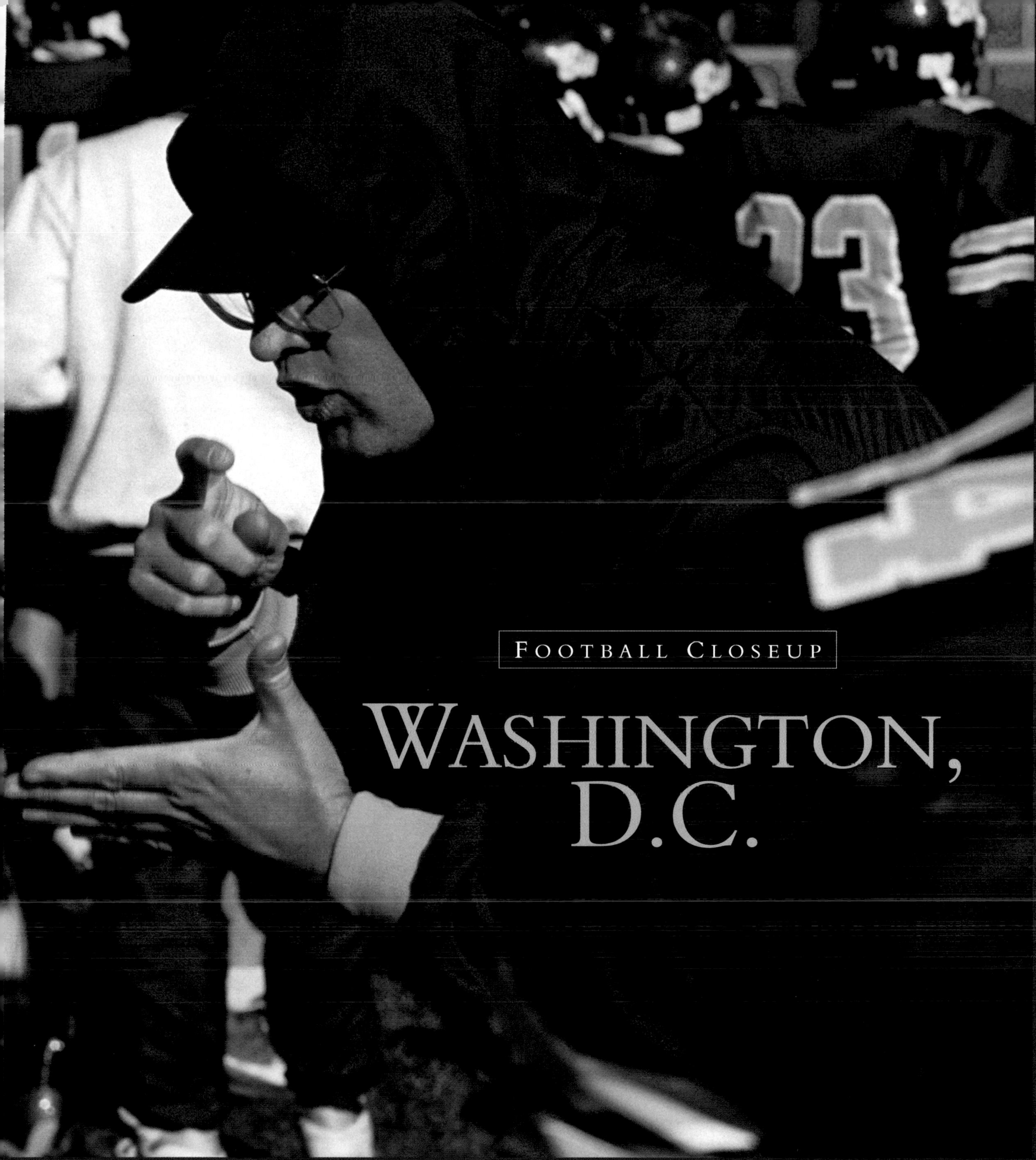

FOOTBALL CLOSEUP

WASHINGTON, D.C.

deaf players to communicate without the other team seeing the signs.

After college, Hubbard coached at a school for the deaf in Kansas. He used the huddle there and the idea spread to other schools, including major colleges, which found the innovation a more efficient way to call plays.

▲ ASSISTANT COACH MARK TESSIER USES SIGN LANGUAGE TO CONVEY HIS INSTRUCTIONS.

Gallaudet, located in Washington, D.C., a short distance from the nation's capitol, is proud of its unique place in football history. It is proud of the fact that its team, with a handful of recruits and

THE VIBRATION OF A BASS DRUM SIGNALS THE SNAP COUNT.

walk-ons, still competes against schools with athletes who are not hearing-impaired. Gallaudet's full-time student enrollment is 2,200.

"Our students want to show the people in the hearing world they can do everything the rest of the world can do, except hear," Gallaudet coach Rich Pelletier says. "Competing in sports, especially a very demanding sport like football, is one way to express that."

That feeling is summed up in a sign that hangs in the Gallaudet locker room: "We Are All Alike. We Have Eyes, Ears, Arms, Legs, and a Head. The Difference Is in the Heart."

Gallaudet's coaches and players communicate through sign language and lip-reading. Pelletier's pregame pep talks are as passionate as those of any other college coach; the only difference is Pelletier delivers his talk with his hands.

When he asks, "Do you want to win?" the players respond with a high-pitched wail that echoes off the locker-room walls. There are no words, or even a distinct pitch, yet the emotion of the players is clear and powerful.

On the field, a bass drum provides the snap count for the offense. Because the players can't hear the quarterback, a team manager supplies the cadence by pounding the drum. The players, who can feel the vibration, identify the snap count by the beat of the drum.

"We wouldn't know what to do without the drum," Pelletier says. "Before we started using it [1970], the players had to line up with their heads pointing toward the ball. They couldn't move until they saw the ball move and that delayed everything. With the drum, they feel the count and off they go."

When the home team scores, instead of applauding, the Gallaudet fans hold their hands over their heads and wiggle their fingers. The student body has continued to support the team, even though it has managed only four winning seasons since 1930.

"There is a lot of spirit in this school," says Pelletier, who is a Gallaudet graduate and football letter-winner. "Homecoming is very important here. There is always a big alumni turnout, and what would homecoming be without football?"

Around the turn of the century, the Gallaudet team was a match for most Eastern colleges. The Bison defeated Navy, Virginia, Villanova, and Maryland, among other schools. In 1913, Gallaudet was 6-1, including a 47-7 victory over Wake Forest.

But as time passed, college football became more competitive and Gallaudet could not keep up. The Bison competed at the Division III level

for a time, then became an independent. Gallaudet now plays schools such as Catholic University and Hartwick College, which have club teams.

With no scholarships to offer and a small talent pool from which to draw, the Gallaudet football program struggles for every victory. From 1990 through 1995, the Bison won 5 games, lost 48, and tied 1.

Losing frustrates the coaches and players, but Pelletier, who has been on campus as a student, teacher, and coach for 25 years, keeps things in perspective.

"I tell the team one thing: Keep working," Pelletier says. "We had to leave Division III because we kept losing and there was no way to

Rich Pelletier (jacket) and his Bison are part of a century-old Gallaudet tradition.

▲ School spirit never has sagged, even after only five victories in six seasons.

build confidence in that situation.

"We keep trying. As coaches, we focus on the areas where we have improved. We may lose a game, but if we played well in the second half, that is what we point to. We build on that.

"We have disadvantages, obviously, because the number of deaf students playing football across the country is very small. Some boys who come out for our team never played in high school. We don't cut anyone. If they have an interest, we nurture it.

"These players love the game. I think they become better people by playing it. They mature and develop leadership skills. To see that is the fun part of coaching."

32
JOSEPH 32
Wilson

see the losers spiking their helmets and gazing morosely at the ground on the other sideline, and you have to sympathize with them because they are you. And that might be the hardest thing to grasp in all of sports, harder than all the variations and options in Bill Walsh's West Coast offense. On an individual level, there isn't a whole lot separating the winner from the loser. Usually it's a matter of having more talented teammates or better coaching. At most, it's the ability to focus clearly on a given night; at the least it's simple luck. So the athlete learns to live with victory and defeat, incorporating them into his or her self-image rather than riding them up and down like an out-of-control pogo stick. But what about the fan? We invest a lot in our football teams, probably more than we'd care to admit. A 3-8 season can make for the longest, dreariest autumn. It can make winter seem like a cheerful change of pace. A victory on Saturday or Sunday can put an entire city in a good mood for most of a week. The computer programmers and the drywallers actually offer one another parking spots. But why? Why are the Falcons and the Spartans and the Fighting Quakers so important to us? It isn't really our bond with the players, though we might tell ourselves it is. The high school and college lineups change every two or three years, and in the age of free agency, pro rosters turn over almost as quickly. No, it's the colors and the logo and the team name we identify with. That's not a very flattering assessment. It puts us on equal footing with the military zealot and the gang member. But it is human nature, and there are good associations with team loyalty, too. If your father took you to games at War Memorial Stadium, and you grew up rooting for Jack Kemp and Cookie Gilchrist, you still root for the Bills, except now you take your kid to Rich Stadium to cheer for Jim Kelly and Thurman Thomas. There is something true in that. We need winners and losers. Most of us drive to jobs where our work is rated subjectively, if at all. When we are praised or chastised, it doesn't always bear any relation to how we think we have performed. Football gives us clear results. It gives us yardage lines to measure our gains. It attaches a value to our touchdowns. It lets us point a finger at the guy who fumbled on the goal line and say, "You blew it for us! It's your fault!" And it gives us a chance to applaud our heroes and, occasionally, to say, "We're number one." You can read it on the scoreboard, you can see it in the standings, right there in black-and-white. It is honest, and we need that once in a while.

▲ Graceland College hits the jackpot against William Jewell. Liberty, Missouri.

◀ Qadry Ismail gets a consoling embrace after a Vikings loss. Minneapolis, Minnesota.

THE UNIVERSITY OF WASHINGTON
REJOICES AFTER A TOUCHDOWN.
SEATTLE, WASHINGTON.

An injured player at Key West, Florida, High School laments his fate.

The walk is longer
when you lose.
South Kendall, Florida.

A DIRTY SHAME.
CLOVIS, CALIFORNIA.

YOUNTZ
54

Nice game, Guys. The Lewisville, North Carolina, Titans.

USAir
Wilson

To the victors go the smiles: The Flemington, New Jersey, Falcons.

30
70
25

After the battle: Jefferson High meets Lee High. Fairfax, Virginia.

Raised Helmets salute Harvard's victory over Yale. New Haven, Connecticut.

ment, pay for their own insurance, and tape their own ankles before games.

The players also chip in for expenses, such as lighting the field for practice and fueling the vans for away games. It costs each man a few hundred dollars over the course of a season.

"It's still cheaper than golf, or going to a movie every weekend," Blechen says. "I'd pay twice that amount just for the opportunity to play."

"It takes a special kind of person to play at this level because there are so many headaches," says Ventura coach Bo Brooks. "The way Bob keeps going year after year and never loses his enthusiasm is amazing."

Blechen is often amused by the reaction of strangers who find out that he plays football. Most assume he plays touch football, probably with other men his age.

When Blechen tells them it is fully dressed tackle football and most of the players are in their twenties and thirties, they look at him as if he were crazy.

"They say, 'That can't be.' I say, 'Come out Sunday and watch,'" says Blechen, who is a sturdily built 6 feet 5 inches and 280 pounds. "I'm sure they think I'm deranged, and maybe I am, a little.

"Over the years, some players have said things like, 'Hey, Pops, when are you gonna retire?' I tell them I'll play longer than they will. They laugh, but I look around now and most of them are gone. I'm still playing.

"I've always thought of myself as young. I was the youngest in my family. I skipped a grade in school, so I was the youngest there. In college, I was the youngest player to make varsity. I got used to thinking young. I guess it carried over."

On the field, with his helmet concealing his bald head and weathered face, Blechen looks like any other weekend warrior in the Pacific Football League. He certainly doesn't look like a man with five grown children and 10 grandchildren.

Most of the players in the Pacific Football League are former high school and small-college stars who weren't quite big enough or fast enough for pro football, but still want to play.

They need the competition, the contact, the adrenalin rush that comes with strapping on the gear and playing the game.

There are all kinds in the league: construction workers, lawyers, mail carriers, bartenders, truck drivers, parole officers, and parolees. Football is the one thing they all have in common.

The game may be even more dangerous at this level than in the National Football League because here the skill levels differ so widely and many players fly around the field out of control. Late hits and scuffles are commonplace.

Blechen serves as an island of calm. A soft-spoken man, he rarely shows emotion on the field. When the game ends, he shakes his opponent's hand and leads both teams in prayer.

He always finishes the same way: "Thank you, Lord, for allowing us to play the greatest game on earth."

In the 1995 season, Blechen started every game, either at center or tackle. He played both ways, offense and defense, in two games when Ventura was short on players. He more than held his own against opponents who were half his age.

"If I didn't play alongside the guy, I wouldn't believe it," says Tony Downs, a guard and Blechen's teammate for five seasons. At 28, Downs is younger than three of Blechen's five children.

"The first time I saw him, I thought he was a coach. Then I saw him put on the pads, and I thought it was some kind of joke. Then I saw him play and it was, like, 'Wow, he is good.'

"Sometimes during games, when I'm hurting or tired, I'll look over at Bob and think, 'How does he do it?' The man is an inspiration to me…to all of us."

"I'm not going to overpower these younger guys, so I use my experience," says Blechen, who played at Whittier (California) College and spent the 1956 preseason with the NFL's Detroit Lions.

"I see where my opponent lines up, what he likes to do. Does he come inside or go outside? I adjust my blocking angles and cut him off. I play a finesse game. It saves wear and tear on my body.

BIKE
99
MAXPRO
22
23

▲ Blechen (99) gets kiddded about his age, but he keeps outlasting teammates.

"God has blessed me with a body that doesn't need a lot of conditioning. I know they say you get more brittle and heal more slowly as you get older, but I haven't found that to be the case. "I feel wonderful. I'm enjoying life more now than I did when I was in my thirties. Staying active and playing ball is part of that."

A younger Blechen often played for more than one team in a season. He would play two games some weekends and squeeze in a third if, as often happens in sandlot ball, he got a call from a team

searching for a fill-in at the last minute.

Blechen also played in spring leagues, which meant he played nine months out of 12. In recent years, he played with a Christian-ministry team that traveled abroad and played exhibition games in Finland, Bulgaria, and the former Soviet Union.

Blechen estimates he has played some 500 games in his career. By all accounts, he has played more minutes of organized football than anyone who ever lived.

He is the game's all-time iron man, although few people outside the Pacific Football League know his name. In 1990, he was inducted into the American Football Association Hall of Fame in Bensonville, Illinois, which honors semipro and minor-league players.

The only other 60-year-old who is known to have played is former Yale All-America William (Pudge) Heffelfinger in the 1930s. Heffelfinger scrimmaged with the Eli varsity in his later years and played in a few charity games, but that was after he was retired for some time.

Blechen has played almost continuously since 1949. To put that in context, he has been in a three-point stance since Harry Truman was in the White House.

Blechen has been asked hundreds of times for the secret of his longevity.

A rigorous fitness program? Not really. He lifts weights and runs a bit in the offseason, but it is all done in moderation.

A physical job? Hardly. Blechen, an honors graduate of Whittier with a degree in chemistry, has worked at a desk most of his life.

Blechen's career is even more remarkable when you consider he had a mild case of polio as a boy and was told he might never play sports.

In 1986, at 51, Blechen was diagnosed with bladder cancer. He underwent surgery during a football offseason and rejoined the Cardinals the following year.

"It's all in your frame of mind," Blechen says. "With me, it's a matter of belief. I believe I can do it, so I do it.

"I put things on a scale, mentally, and if it tilts heavily to the good, I say go for it. Some people never climb a mountain. They look at it and say it's too hard. But look at the reward. When you get to the top, it's exhilarating. It's worth the pain.

"That's how I feel about football. After a game, I'm hot, dirty, and sweaty, probably a little scraped and sore, but so what? I love it. Win or lose, I love playing."

Blechen played both offense and defense at Whittier under coach George Allen, who later gained fame with the Los Angeles Rams and Washington Redskins in the NFL.

"Blechen used to run like he had a piano on his back, but he was the smartest player I ever coached," Allen once said.

Blechen was drafted by the Lions in 1956 and was one of the last cuts from a powerful Detroit team that included four future Pro Football Hall of Fame enshrinees.

He played one season in the Canadian Football League, then moved to California to pursue a business career. He was not ready to give up football altogether, however, so he joined a semipro team, the Eagle Rock Athletic Club.

Eagle Rock was a powerhouse that attracted the best players in the area. The team did not lose a game for seven seasons and twice scrimmaged the Dallas Cowboys when the Cowboys were training on the West Coast in the early sixties.

But even winning teams such as Eagle Rock had trouble surviving as the NFL flourished and the sandlot leagues dried up. It was hard to keep teams going as operating costs soared and the older players, who were the backbone of the semipro game, retired.

Blechen joined Ventura in the late 1980s. At the time, the team had several players with at least some NFL experience, including quarterback Kevin Hicks, who spent a preseason with the Cowboys.

By 1995, most of those players were gone, and the Cardinals had trouble just putting a team on the field. Brooks, the coach and general manager, never knew which players would show up from one week to the next.

Blechen was the one constant. He never missed a game or practice. He followed the same ritual: listening to tapes of John Philip Sousa and the Mormon Tabernacle Choir while driving to the field. The music helped Blechen get in a football frame of mind.

Ventura played its home games on a dusty field at a naval base. The players dressed in a building with broken windows. The bleachers were nearly empty except for a few friends and relatives, including Blechen's wife Joan.

Joan Blechen does not particularly like football. She never watched the game before

meeting Bob. Yet she has backed him throughout his career, and she still greets him with a hug and kiss after each game when he comes off the field.

"I appreciate his love of the game," she says. "I admire him for being able to do what he has done. "

The Cardinals won only two games in 1995. It would be a bad season for most people, but not Blechen. In his view, there are no bad football seasons. He cherishes them all.

"I've been so lucky just to play this long," Blechen says. "I was disappointed when I didn't make it with the Lions. I thought, 'Oh, that's so unfair.' But it was for the best.

"If I had made it with Detroit, or in the Canadian League, I would've only lasted one or two years. I wasn't athletic enough to play at that level.

"And I probably would not have played semi-pro ball later. I would've just walked away from the game. I would've missed out on all these years of playing and having fun.

"Even when I lose, I still enjoy the competition. Once I was with a team that lost a game 100-12. It's hard to imagine, but it happened. In a game like that, I focus on one thing and that's my battle with the man across from me.

"I may be on a team that can't win a game; I may be in a game where my team can't make a first down; but I always have that next play. That's what keeps me going."

CHAPTER SEVEN

THE WARRIORS

A long time ago, you could see a football player's face as he lumbered across the field. You knew the players then. You knew them by their toothless smiles, their scars, and their serpentine noses. It's nice to be recognizable, but not *that* recognizable. ✯ Still, some people pine for those eye-gouging days. They claim that the bulky equipment of modern football makes the game too impersonal. The faces are hidden behind helmets and masks, the bodies reshaped by hard foam pads that extend from the neck to the knees. At the novice levels of the sport the players are nameless, or at least their shirts are. ✯ It's a game of robots. Except for one thing: You couldn't get a machine to do what a football player does. Some day they will program a solid-state virtual athlete with the physical and analytical abilities necessary to drive block or read defenses...and still it won't be enough. ✯ A machine is only as good as its engineering. It has definitive, non-negotiable limits. A football player is both better and worse than that. He often falls short of his potential, yes, but sometimes he finds a way to exceed his barriers. A machine can't improve its speed or its power via the force of its own exertion, as players do each summer. A machine can't perform to complete exhaustion, to the edge of breakdown, then somehow find reserve energy when the game goes into overtime. A machine feels no pressure, but it can't feed upon the roar of the crowd and actually pick it up a notch when there's 1:48 on the clock and the end zone is 64 yards away. ✯ Anyway, if a machine could do all that, Don Shula would have signed it to a short-term contract years ago. ✯ So who are these players? Who are the soldiers so willing to lose themselves in the anonymity of a football uniform? ✯ There's a skinny high school junior and Sega junkie who quit his job at the car wash to join the varsity team. The spending money will be sparse now, but if he helps his dad lay concrete on weekends, he can make it work. He's really not one of the better players on the team, but the coach, who also happens to be his biology teacher, likes to put him on special teams because he's damn near fearless. ✯ There's a college sophomore at Colorado who made the team as a walk-on a year ago. He was unrecruited out of high school, but he grabbed the coaches' eyes by catching 50 to 100 passes after practice every day. He'll get a scholarship this year. He's still no star, but he'll see playing time in third-and-long situations. ✯ There's a guard for the Buffalo Bills who blew out his right knee a year ago. At 33, with plenty of money in the bank, he could have called it quits and nobody would have questioned the decision. But there he is, grimacing over leg curls in the weight room before the strength coach even has shown up for work. Something won't let him walk

◄ BATTLE CRY: LAMAR LATHON OF THE CAROLINA PANTHERS.

away from the game. ✯ Every story is different and every personality is distinct, because we're talking about human beings. Still, certain traits seem to carry over from the intramural field to the Superdome. What makes a football player? You can start with the outmoded ideals of persistence and courage. ✯ Every season offers a bounty of opportunities to choose a new occupation. If you're looking for excuses, they're right on the tip of your tongue, which just got split open by the fullback's elbow. A football season is a four-month survival course. It's Outward Bound without the trail mix. Your ankle will swell, your head will ring, and your ribs will throb, and it's considered part of the job description. Your workplace is mud, snow, hardened dirt, and a hostile green carpet that tends to peel skin from your elbows. You will be fooled, berated, and almost certainly defeated, and you are expected to treat it all as a "learning experience." A life such as that tends to breed tough s.o.b.'s, and proud ones. ✯ Another common bond is ego, which, especially at the professional level, often is twisted into fear of failure. ✯ "To me, football is a contest in embarrassments," former NFL defensive tackle Alex Karras once said.

"The quarterback is out there to embarrass me in front of my friends, my teammates, my coaches, my wife, and my three boys. The quarterback doesn't leave me any choice. I've got to embarrass him instead." ✯ There is something even more basic to football than the anxiety described by Karras. There is passion for the game. A football player is a football player at any age, in any league. He is defined not by his accomplishments, but by his self-image. ✯ A sixth-grader's alarm goes off in the morning. He was dreaming about football. He was intercepting a pass, dodging tacklers, and running along the sideline as the masses swooned. Fifteen years later, he's playing in the NFL every Sunday, but every Saturday night his dream is much the same. There is more peril in it now, less freedom, but there is the same exhilaration he always felt as he races to the end zone. ✯ That passion is why the football player can't wait for the season to roll around each year, why he can't bear to walk away from the game, even when the bodies around him are faster and stronger than his. It's why, even after he does quit, he can be coaxed into a sprint by anyone who picks up a ball, nods downfield, and says, "Go long."

▲ A MESSAGE FROM DORSEY HIGH SCHOOL. LOS ANGELES, CALIFORNIA.

◀ THE MICHIGAN WOLVERINES ARRIVE FOR BATTLE. ANN ARBOR, MICHIGAN.

The guys in the trenches:
Douglas County High.
Castle Rock, Colorado.

IT'S TIME
IT'S TIME
AIR
BIKE
Reebok

A steely-eyed lineman
at St. John's University
in Collegeville, Minnesota…

…AND A PINT-SIZED COUNTERPART
IN CENTERVILLE, VIRGINIA.

Grimace and grunt: The Pittsburgh Steelers harden themselves.

UNSCHEDULED LANDING: TEXAS A&M VS. TEXAS. COLLEGE STATION, TEXAS.

Florida greets Florida State. Gainesville, Florida.

On the morning of Christmas Eve in Green Bay, the temperature was 24 degrees with a wind-chill factor of 9. The sky was gray, and a light snow was falling as the parking lots opened at Lambeau Field.

Packers weather.

Ray Nitschke, the Pro Football Hall of Fame linebacker, felt a familiar rush as he made his way through the crowd for the final game of the 1995 regular season. It was as if the clock on Lombardi Avenue had been turned back 30 years.

"All the excitement in the air brought back memories," Nitschke says. "That was how I remember it when we were winning championships in the sixties. It always came down to a game in the cold and snow with everything on the line. That was Packers football.

"It was great to see it back after all those years of losing. It was great to see the older fans, who were there for the championship seasons, mixing with the young fans. It was a long time coming."

It was a classic matchup: two teams, the Packers and Pittsburgh Steelers, both en route to division titles, playing in one of pro football's most storied settings, Lambeau Field, on the final Sunday of the regular season.

It was a day that, with each icy blast of wind, stirred echos of the old line: "On the frozen tundra of Lambeau Field..." It was a day that resonated with images lifted from the Vince Lombardi scrapbook. It was a trip back in time to the days when proud little Green Bay earned the nickname "Titletown."

Call this chapter "A Return to Titletown," because when the Packers defeated the Steelers 24-19 they wrapped up first place in the NFC Central Division with an 11-5 record. It was Green Bay's first outright division championship since 1972.

The game was not decided until the final 11 seconds, when Yancey Thigpen, Pittsburgh's Pro Bowl receiver, let a sure touchdown pass slip through his fingers. Thigpen knelt in the end

▶ NORMALLY UNASSUMING GREEN BAY GOES CRAZY OVER ITS PACKERS.

FOOTBALL CLOSEUP

GREEN BAY, WISCONSIN

zone, his head bowed, while the victorious Packers danced around him.

"That was my Christmas present to Green Bay," Thigpen says.

"We'll take it," says Packers safety LeRoy Butler. "We were due for a break."

When the game ended, quarterback Brett Favre, who was beaten bloody in the second half, and defensive end Reggie White stayed on the field to celebrate with the 60,649 fans. It was such an emotional scene that even losing coach Bill Cowher paused in the tunnel to watch.

"It's great that this city, this field gets to go through this again," Cowher says, aware that Green Bay would host a first-round playoff game the following week. "It was electric out there. It was special. That's what this game is all about."

Pro football was not born in Green Bay, but it seems that way. A working-class town at the mouth of the Fox River, built on paper mills and canning plants, Green Bay has football roots that date to 1919.

Most cities that had teams in the American Professional Football Association—Canton,

◀ A HOME GAME IS AN ALL-DAY EVENT THAT BEGINS WITH A TAILGATING FEAST.

Akron, and Muncie, among others—eventually lost them. Some went bankrupt, others could not compete when the Association reorganized as the National Football League in 1922 and brought the game to the big cities. Green Bay was the one frontier outpost that survived.

With its population of 96,000, Green Bay still is the smallest city with an NFL team. It is dwarfed by the likes of Chicago and New York. Yet Green Bay can claim more league championships (11) than any other franchise in professional football.

"The Cowboys call themselves America's Team, but I really think the Packers are America's Team," says Nitschke, who anchored Green Bay's defense from 1958 through 1972. "This is a country where the little guy gets to compete with the big guy. That's what Green Bay has done. That's what the whole franchise is about."

The franchise was founded by Earl (Curly) Lambeau, who was a player, coach, and part-owner. Lambeau talked his employer, the Indian Packing Company, into putting up $500 for equipment and allowing him to use the company grounds for practice. For that, Lambeau agreed to call his team the Packers.

The Indian Packing Company went out of business within a year, but the team endured, and its legend grew. The Packers won six league titles under Lambeau (1929-1931, 1936, 1939, 1944) and five under Lombardi (1961-62, 1965-67), including Super Bowls I and II.

The franchise almost went under in 1933, when a fan won a suit for $25,000 after falling from the temporary stands at City Stadium. The two companies that had insured the team failed. For a time, the Packers were in receivership. The club was saved by a fund-raising drive in which local residents bought shares in the team.

▶ EVEN THE NEW GENERATION OF FANS KNOWS ABOUT PACKERS TRADITION.

Today, there are 4,634 shares of Green Bay Packers, Inc., owned by 1,898 shareholders. Most are regular working folks: merchants, bus drivers, salesmen. They are in it for one reason: love of the game. Packers shareholders receive no dividends, and by rule, all profits are poured back into the team. That is how the Packers could afford to build a $4 million indoor practice facility and pay $17 million for a free agent such as Reggie White.

The Packers are the only publicly owned team in the NFL.

When one of the Packers scores a touchdown and dives into the crowd behind the end zone at Lambeau Field—the move was popularized by receiver Robert Brooks in 1995—it symbolizes the unique bond that exists between the team and the community in Green Bay.

In most NFL cities, that would sound hopelessly old-fashioned. But in Green Bay, where the city flag features a roll of paper, a wedge of cheese, and a Packers helmet, it is as real today as it was a half century ago when Lambeau won his last championship.

There are 37 businesses in town with the word "Pack" or "Packers" in their names. The middle

GREEN BAY FANS STAND ALONE WHEN IT COMES TO COLORFUL COSTUMES AND ANIMATED SUPPORT OF THEIR TEAM.

school is named after Vince Lombardi, and one of the late coach's locker-room speeches is bronzed and hangs in the school cafeteria.

When the Packers went to the playoffs in 1995, the townspeople tied green and gold ribbons around trees and telephone poles. Hundreds of people, from bank tellers to truck drivers, wore Packers jerseys to work. It was like a college town on homecoming weekend. Everyone was caught up in the spirit.

The intimacy of Green Bay makes people feel close to the team. A fan in Philadelphia or New York has a million-in-one chance of ever bumping into a player on the street. But in Green Bay, you never know when Brett Favre might sit next to you in the movies or LeRoy Butler might walk down the same aisle in the supermarket.

Only in Green Bay will you find players riding bicycles from the practice field back to the locker room, while the youngsters who own the bikes run alongside, carrying their heroes' helmets.

"It is refreshing to see what we have here," says tackle Ken Ruettgers, who completed his eleventh season in Green Bay in 1995. "Most places, there is a gap between the fans and players. [The fans] cheer for the team, but they don't connect emotionally the way they do here."

Originally, Ruettgers was not thrilled at the prospect of playing in Green Bay. An All-America at Southern California, he cringed when the Packers selected him in the 1985 draft. The Packers were a mediocre team that played in a harsh climate, reasons enough to make the California native wish he could find a way out.

"If there was free agency then, I would've been gone," Ruettgers says. "My first seven years in Green Bay, we didn't make the playoffs once. I was ready to get out."

It wasn't just the losing that gnawed at Ruettgers. It also was living with the ghosts of the past. Everywhere a player turns in Green Bay, he is reminded of the Lombardi dynasty. Nitschke still is a visible presence. Fuzzy Thurston, the former guard, owns a bar in town.

Gary Knafelc, a former tight end, is the public-address announcer at Lambeau Field.

The glory of the championship years only magnified the shortcomings of the teams from 1973 through 1991, a period in which the Packers had three winning seasons and went to the playoffs only once.

The franchise drifted aimlessly until 1991 when the seven-man executive committee that runs the team hired Ron Wolf as executive vice president and general manager. Wolf, in turn, hired Mike Holmgren, then an assistant coach with San Francisco, as head coach and traded for Favre, then a backup in Atlanta.

Those moves, coupled with the signing of White the following year, put the Packers back on track. The team, which did not have back-to-back winning seasons for almost 30 years, had three consecutive 9-7 finishes under Holmgren before improving to 11-5 in 1995.

Favre matured into one of the game's premier quarterbacks. In 1995, he passed for an NFC record 38 touchdowns and was named the league's most valuable player. A small-town boy from Kiln, Mississippi (population 7,500), Favre feels at home in Green Bay.

White's signing was a watershed moment for the Packers. An all-pro with the Philadelphia Eagles, White was the most hotly pursued free agent of 1993. He had offers to sign in a dozen cities, yet he chose Green Bay.

White's decision accomplished two things: It immediately improved the Packers' defense, and it dispelled the notion that Green Bay could not compete with the richer and more glamorous NFL cities for quality free agents.

"Getting Reggie brought us instant credibility," Wolf says.

White said he was drawn to the Packers by their proud tradition and by the challenge of building a new dynasty in Green Bay to take its place alongside those built by Lambeau and Lombardi.

Favre worried for a time about suffocating in the shadow of Hall of Fame quarterback Bart

A LOT WAS AT STAKE FOR THE PACKERS, AS STEELERS RUNNING BACK TIM LESTER DISCOVERED.

THE STEELERS, BOUND FOR SUPER BOWL XXX, WERE IN THE GAME UNTIL THE END.

Starr and the other Packers legends. But in 1995, Favre led the Packers within one game of Super Bowl XXX.

"Each year, I hear more about our team and less about the past," he says. "What those [Lombardi] guys did was fantastic, but thirty years from now, we want people to say, 'Boy, those Packers of the nineties were really great.' We want to be thought of in the same way.

"The only way we can do that is to win championships and [1995] was a start. We lost some key guys, we had some injuries that really hurt us, but we pulled together and kept going. We really grew as a team."

This is a new generation of Packers and, to a large extent, a new generation of fans. Many of the current ticket holders are sons and daughters of fans who attended the Ice Bowl, the legendary 1967 NFL Championship Game, in which the Packers defeated Dallas 21-17 on a day when the temperature fell to 16 degrees below zero.

It is a younger, more boisterous group of fans than those who filled the seats then. In the Lombardi era, the fans wore parkas and ski masks. Today, they wear fake blocks of cheese on their heads and paint their bodies green and gold. Some wear Packers helmets adorned with elk horns and Christmas lights.

It is a colorful setting, loud and lively, yet still polite in a Green Bay kind of way. The security guards at Lambeau Field eject spectators for swearing. Toss a snowball and you lose your season ticket. (There are 20,000 people on the waiting list for Packers season tickets, so you won't be missed.)

The atmosphere outside Lambeau Field before a game, with its lavish tailgating and carving of football ice sculptures, is so rich that in his first visit Kansas City Chiefs owner Lamar Hunt walked the full perimeter of the stadium, taking in the sights.

"There's an aura here that nobody else has," Hunt says.

"I always think of that stadium as being everything that's good about football," says television analyst John Madden, a former Raiders coach. "There are things you get to hate after a while, like artificial turf and domed stadiums. Then you get to Lambeau Field, and there is something fresh about it."

▲ The Packers barely held on to Fred McAfee—and to the division title.

The Christmas Eve game against Pittsburgh had the look and feel of a vintage afternoon in Green Bay. It was a critical game for the Packers because a loss would have given Detroit the division title and sent the Packers into the playoffs as a wild-card team that had to play its games on the road.

Winning the Central Division championship meant an opening-round game at home. The Packers had won 16 of their previous 17 games at

TEAMMATES MUGGED MARK CHMURA AFTER A TOUCHDOWN RECEPTION.

▲ Crowd favorite Reggie White was engulfed by fans after the victory.

Lambeau Field and were perfect (8-0) at home in the postseason.

Talking to the team before the game, Holmgren did not have to belabor the obvious. If the Packers wanted to make a serious run at the Super Bowl, they had to defeat a Steelers team that had an eight-game winning streak.

White played despite an injured hamstring. Brooks played with a separated shoulder and caught 11 passes for 137 yards and a touchdown. It was a bruising game, a three-hour battle in the mud and the blowing snow.

Favre was sent to the sidelines twice, once when he was hit by safety Myron Bell and began spitting up blood and, later, when he was dazed on a tackle by linebacker Kevin Greene.

Favre did not miss a snap as a result of the first injury, which doctors termed a bruised chest. After calling a time out, he threw a touchdown pass to tight end Mark Chmura on the next play. Greene's hit sent Favre to the sideline for two plays, but he returned to finish the game.

"It was scary to see Brett in that condition, especially when he was spitting up all that blood," Ruettgers says. "I thought for sure when he went to the bench, he was done for the day. When he came back, I couldn't believe it. Then he threw a touchdown pass on the next play. It was like comic-book hero stuff, but that's Brett."

"Never in my life have I spit up blood that badly," Favre says. "The doctors thought it was a punctured lung at first. They were checking me out and I said, 'Hey, guys, I'm not coming out, not with the ball on the one-yard line.' I basically put myself back in the game and threw the pass to Mark.

"When Greene hit me, it knocked me goofy. I sat on the bench, got a drink, and let the fog clear. By the time we got the ball back, I was okay. It was like a street fight that day. Both teams were pounding on each other. When it was over, I was sore from head to foot.

"But I got to put on one of those hats that said 'NFC Central Division Champs.' All the pain went away."

AFC showdown: The Steelers have their hands full with the Colts. Pittsburgh, Pennsylvania.

TRADITION REVISITED: HARVARD COLLIDES WITH YALE. NEW HAVEN, CONNECTICUT.

THE CITRUS BOWL: OHIO STATE MAKES MUSIC AT HALFTIME…

…And Tennessee makes yardage late in the game. Orlando, Florida.

HEAD-BUTTING RIVALS:
UCLA AND USC.
LOS ANGELES, CALIFORNIA.

TEXAS A&M STREAKS INTO
COMBAT WITH TEXAS.
COLLEGE STATION, TEXAS.

QUALITY PLUS
FORD
DEALERS
ARMY NAVY

A RITUAL WORTH CELEBRATING: ARMY VS. NAVY.
PHILADELPHIA, PENNSYLVANIA.

Diana Ross wows the crowd at halftime of Super Bowl XXX.

FOOTBALL CLOSEUP

TEMPE, ARIZONA

Troy Aikman has played football most of his life. He played both at the University of Oklahoma and UCLA. He was the first pick in the 1989 NFL draft, a rookie starter with the Dallas Cowboys, an athlete whose career profile defines big time.

Aikman had played in many high-stakes games, he had played before huge crowds—the Rose Bowl, with its 103,000 seats, was his home field at UCLA—and he knew all about pressure. At least that was what he thought.

Then he went on the field for his first Super Bowl and realized, to his amazement, he could not breathe. He said the atmosphere in the stadium that day seemed to suck all the air from his body.

"I was hyperventilating in the huddle. I thought I was going to pass out," the Dallas quarterback says. "I'd never felt anything like that before."

That is what the Super Bowl does to its players. Before it makes them rich, before it sends

COUNTDOWN TO KICKOFF: SUPER BOWL MORNING AT SUN DEVIL STADIUM.

them off to Disney World or delivers them to the Pro Football Hall of Fame, it takes their breath away. It makes their knees shake, if only for the first few minutes when the jets thunder over the stadium, the fireworks explode, and suddenly there is the realization: *Hey, this is it.*

"You try to collect your thoughts and settle down, but it's hard," Aikman says. "This is the Super Bowl. It's the game you dreamed about playing all your life. You can't expect it to feel like any other game because it's not."

Indeed, the Super Bowl is a game unlike any other. It is a spectacle played out on a global stage. It is an event that, for a few hours on a Sunday in January, glows at the center of every living room, bar room, and board room in America. It is, quite simply, *The Game.*

When a player rises to that occasion—as Aikman did in Super Bowl XXVII, throwing 4 touchdown passes and winning most-valuable-player honors in the victory over the Bills—he is assured a lasting place in football history. When he doesn't, he has to live with that, too. Ask Buffalo quarterback Jim Kelly, who was on the losing side in that Super Bowl and three others—XXV, XXVI, and XXVIII.

There are no small successes in the Super Bowl nor are there any little failures. Everything that goes on—from the lavish pregame parties to the high-concept television commercials—makes the event and its players seem larger than life.

▲ THE MEDIA ARE PART OF THE SPECTACLE, AS THE STEELERS' GREG LLOYD LEARNED.

The Super Bowl is America at its best and worst. It is loud and overdressed and self-important, but it also is human and honest and passionate in a way that touches us all. "The Super Bowl," wrote Norman Chad in *TV Guide*, "has become Main Street's Mardi Gras."

Aikman was back for his third Super Bowl appearance in January, 1996, when the Cowboys defeated the Pittsburgh Steelers 27-17 in Super Bowl XXX. And the event, which some people said could not get any bigger, did exactly that in its first trip to Arizona.

The game, played at Sun Devil Stadium in Tempe, was the most-watched program in television history. The NBC network estimated its U.S. audience at 138,488,000. The previous record was 134,800,000 viewers for the Dallas-Buffalo matchup in Super Bowl XXVIII. The four largest TV audiences of all-time—and eight of the top 10—are Super Bowls.

Those numbers, impressive as they are, represent just a fraction of the game's true audience. Super Bowl XXX also was televised overseas in 18 languages. The radio call was heard in more than 175 countries and territories. For the first time, the game was broadcast in Navajo so the Native American population in Arizona could share in the state's big moment.

It is believed a billion people watched or heard at least part of the game on TV or radio. It may have been the wee hours of Monday morning for the Super Bowl parties in Europe, but it still was "Prime Time" whenever Deion Sanders, the Cowboys' cornerback and wide receiver, touched the football.

Super Bowl XXX generated an estimated $200 million in business during its week in Arizona. There were 106 Super Bowl-related events—from celebrity donkey races to The NFL Experience—and they were attended by more than 1.5 million people.

"People want to be part of [Super Bowl] week any way they can," says Michael Irvin, the Cowboys' Pro Bowl receiver. "This is 'The Show.' Players say our goal is to get here. Looks like it's everybody else's goal, too."

It wasn't always this way. The first Super Bowl, played in January, 1967, between Green Bay and Kansas City, drew 61,946 fans to the Los Angeles Coliseum. It was only the fourth-largest crowd to see a football game in the Coliseum that season, trailing one Los Angeles Rams game and two home games for Southern California.

For that Super Bowl, the top ticket price was $12. An hour before kickoff, scalpers were selling them for $6 just to cut their losses. For Super

◀ THE ALWAYS-LAVISH PREGAME ENTERTAINMENT TOOK ON THE COLORS OF THE SOUTHWEST.
▶ BUT THE NATIONAL ANTHEM, PERFORMED BY VANESSA WILLIAMS, WAS THOROUGHLY RED, WHITE, AND BLUE.

Bowl XXX, the cheapest ticket cost $200, the best seats went for $350, and scalpers were getting many times the face value.

The growth of the Super Bowl from its origin as just a championship football game to what it is today—a kind of social and corporate phenomenon—is one of the most remarkable cultural stories of the century.

Pete Rozelle, the former commissioner of the National Football League, is credited with creating and developing the spectacle. But even Rozelle, visionary that he was, never imagined the game would become a mega-event, with more limousines per square inch than the VIP lot at the Academy Awards.

It did not happen all at once. Most people point to Joe Namath and the New York Jets' stunning upset victory in Super Bowl III as the launching pad. But one game and one swaggering quarterback did not make the Super Bowl the marketing juggernaut it is today.

The event grew through a confluence of

◀ THE DALLAS COWBOYS CHEERLEADERS WERE ON HAND TO LEND THEIR SUPPORT.

Today, a 30-second commercial spot during a Super Bowl telecast commands $1.1 million. That is nearly four times what it cost to advertise during the 1995 World Series.

The event continues to grow, even though the games themselves have not always been competitive. Following a string of AFC victories in the seventies, the NFC has dominated the Super Bowl in the eighties and nineties, winning the last 12 games, only two of which were decided by fewer than 10 points.

Yet the TV ratings continue to rise and the cash register swells. Why?

Good planning, for one thing. It was Rozelle's idea to move the game from early January to late in the month to allow interest to build. The Super Bowl now falls a full month after Christmas and almost four weeks after New Year's Day, when most of the country is feeling the winter blues. The Super Bowl gives people a reason to have a party.

It really doesn't matter if the game is competitive: Millions of people still enjoy the party. It gives them something to talk about, something to share, and yes, something to bet on. An estimated $3 billion is wagered, most of it illegally, on each Super Bowl.

Another factor in the game's continued growth is its expanding role as a corporate destination.

forces: the increasing popularity of pro football, the dynamic growth in the media with all-news cable TV networks and 24-hour sports channels, and major corporations awakening to the concept of sports marketing.

Each of those forces was at work, gaining momentum through the 1970s. They merged, to their mutual benefit, in the Super Bowl. It was the right game in the right place at the right time.

▶ DEION (PRIME TIME) SANDERS WAS AT HOME IN THE SUPER BOWL SPOTLIGHT.

▶ Caution, men at work: Emmitt Smith follows the blocks of massive escorts.

Most major companies find some way to tap into the Super Bowl, setting up hospitality tents at the stadium to entertain clients and using trips to the game as an incentive for employees to break sales records.

The larger the event becomes, the harder the sociologists work at explaining it. One theory is that, in an increasingly secular world, the Super Bowl has replaced traditional religious holidays as an event to which people are drawn.

"Sports is a primary refuge from meaninglessness," Dallas Willard, a University of Southern California professor, said in a *Los Angeles Times* interview. "As society has become increasingly unmanageable by the individual, it has called for these massive social expressions…in which we see ourselves and identify ourselves."

The issue may be, as the academics suggest,

▲ Ready, aim…Steelers quarterback Neil O'Donnell targets a receiver.

rooted deep in our collective psyche.

Then again, it may be as simple as this: The Super Bowl is one game to decide an entire season. It is not a best-of-seven series. It is not a drama that will leave you hanging at the end of the night.

It is one game for the championship of professional football. No ties, no polls, no ambiguity. Just a winner and loser. We can make sense of that. That's why there are 3,000 accredited media representatives at the Super Bowl churning out 10-million words of copy during the week.

"The game has gotten so big and the pressure is so great, I think it impacts how some teams play," says Len Dawson, the former Kansas City quarterback who was the MVP of Super Bowl IV and now covers the game as a television reporter.

"It's like the Golden Gloves. The kids are

AN INSPIRED STEELERS' DEFENSE SURRENDERED YARDAGE GRUDGINGLY.

VICTORY MARCH:
THE COWBOYS EXIT
SUN DEVIL STADIUM
IN TRIUMPH.

limited the Cowboys to just 61 total yards in the second half.

"We studied their defense on film, and we knew they were good," says Aikman, who completed 15 of 23 passes for 209 yards and 1 touchdown, a 3-yard pass to tight end Jay Novacek.

"They do a lot of different things—twists, stunts, bringing linebackers in different gaps. We had some luck against them early [Dallas scored on its first three possessions] but we could never seem to get away from them after that."

Pittsburgh's defense clamped down on Smith, who led the NFL with 1,773 rushing yards and 25 touchdowns during the season. Smith had a 23-yard run in the game's first series, but he was held to 26 yards on 17 carries the rest of the day.

The game came down to one crucial series. With 4:15 remaining, the Steelers had the ball at their own 32-yard line, trailing by 3 points. They had momentum on their side and were in position to take the lead and quite possibly win the game with a touchdown.

PROFESSIONAL FOOTBALL'S BIGGEST PRIZE: THE VINCE LOMBARDI TROPHY.

Instead, quarterback Neil O'Donnell threw his second interception of the game to Dallas cornerback Larry Brown, who returned the ball to Pittsburgh's 6-yard line. Moments later, Smith crossed the goal line from 4 yards out to score the touchdown that insured the result.

Brown was voted the game's most valuable player, the first defensive player to receive the honor since Chicago end Richard Dent in Super Bowl XX. It was a bittersweet moment for Brown, who still was mourning the death of his infant son, who was born prematurely, in November.

"Whenever you have a tragedy like that, it stays on your mind," Brown says. "But you have to move on."

Dallas equaled San Francisco's record for most Super Bowl victories, five. But the Cowboys' feat of winning three Super Bowls in four years is unprecedented and they are the only team to win Super Bowls under three different head coaches: Tom Landry, Jimmy Johnson, and Switzer.

"Certainly, this football team has made its place in history," Aikman says. "It has done things that never were done before, and that's very rewarding to all of us.

"Each [Super Bowl] has been a little different. The first one was by far the most fun. It was all new, we didn't know what to expect. It was just enjoyable because there wasn't so much pressure. The second one was rewarding because we did it back-to-back when no one thought that was possible.

"All along, I've felt this team overcame more than the other two teams did because we had so many changes and controversies. It's a very rewarding feeling. It's a sense of relief for all of us. Now we've got two weeks to enjoy this thing, then everybody will be asking: 'Are you going to do it back-to-back again?'

"It's a vicious cycle."